UNBOUND

MW00386788

A MECHWARRIOR ADVENTURE

FASA CORPORATION

CREDITS • CONTENTS

UNBOUND

Writing
Mike Nystul
Blaine Pardoe

Development
Mike "Hi, I'm from Space!" Nystul

Editorial Staff
Senior Editor
Donna Ippolito
Assistant Editor
Sharon Turner Mulvihill

Production Staff
Art Director
Knute, son of Erling
Cover Art
Jeffrey Von Laubenstein
Cover Design
Dr. Laubenstein
Illustration
Rick Harris
Dana Knutson
The Laubenstein
Tony Szczudlo
Mike "Skuzz-O-Rama" Nielsen
Page Design
Diego Nelson
Layout
Tara Jean A. E. Gallagher
Keyline/Paste-up
Ernie "Rico Suave" Hernandez

BATTLETECH®, 'MECH®, BATTLEMECH®
and MECHWARRIOR® are Registered
Trademarks of FASA Corporation. UNBOUND™ is a
Trademark of FASA Corporation. Copyright © 1991 FASA
Corporation. All Rights Reserved.
Printed in the United States of America.

Published by
FASA Corporation
P.O. Box 6930
Chicago, IL 60680

CONTENTS

INTRODUCTION	4
How to Use This Book	4
Margin-of-Success Tables	5
The Story So Far	5
Plot Synopsis	7
Getting Started	7
EPISODE 1: JOINING UP	10
Making Contact	10
Proving Ground	14
Inside Job	16
EPISODE 2: RISE AND FALL	20
Challenge Match	20
Showdown	24
Intercession	28
EPISODE 3: POWER PLAY	34
Matchmaker	34
Prometheus Unchained	36
Rampage	38
END GAME	42
Awarding Adventure Points	42
Loose Ends	43
RESEARCH	44
CAST OF CHARACTERS	48
The Deadly Sins	48
Kavin Drek	48
Thomas Devon	49
Lorri Barris	50
Diana Hunsaker	51
Avery Hart	52
Other Characters	53
Loucynda Byrd	53
Winston Davis	54
Major Nancy Jerrold	55
Professor Burke Kale	56
Gordon West	57
LOCATIONS	58
The Pelican	58
Characters	60
Deadly Sins Stable	60
The Pit	62
Characters	63
NEW TECH	64
Control Systems	64
Alternative Ordnance	68
New Weapons Systems	71
New Defensive Systems	72
New BattleMechs	73

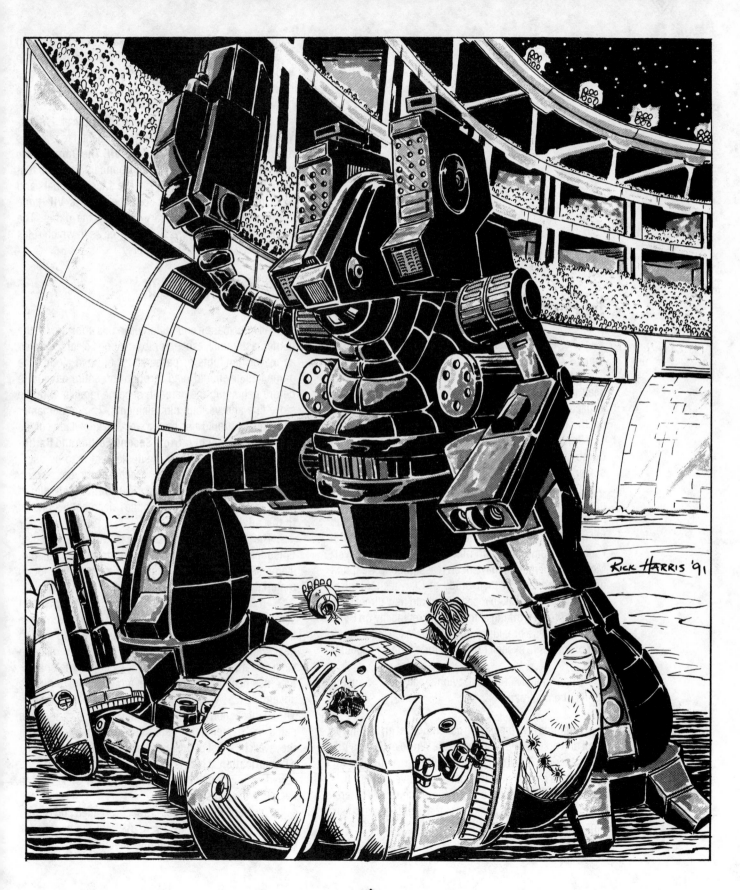

made up of any character type the players choose as long as at least one character is a MechWarrior. In a group with the best chance of successfully completing this mission, half the group will be MechWarriors and the balance will be technicians, traders, and scouts.

Aside from the basic rules of **BattleTech** and **Mech-Warrior, Second Edition**, everything needed to play this adventure is included here. **Solaris VII, The Game World** provides dueling rules and background information that would help the gamemaster run the 'Mech combats and flesh out the Game World, but the **Solaris VII** game supplement is not necessary to enjoy the game. The gamemaster and players should agree as to which rules will be used before beginning play.

HOW TO USE THIS BOOK

All information and materials in this book are for the gamemaster only, except for the sections clearly marked as player handouts or passages to be read aloud. The gamemaster should read through the entire adventure before beginning the game to become familiar with the story line and various plot elements. The gamemaster and players should also have a working knowledge of the basic rules in **MechWarrior, Second Edition** and **Battle-Tech**, and **Solaris VII** if that supplement is to be used. Players who intend to play MechWarrior characters, especially, should be familiar with the **BattleTech** rules in order to compete effectively in the 'Mech battles pivotal to this adventure.

The adventure is presented in three parts called **Episodes**, which divide the adventure into major plot elements. In most cases, an Episode contains enough material for a single gaming session.

An Episode is made up of one or more **Events**, plot elements that move the story forward. Each Event section describes what is happening and why, and how to deal with the decisions the player characters make in each situation in game terms. For example, the characters may need information from a main character in the adventure who is known to hang out at a particular bar. The event section gets the characters to the bar, and then helps the gamemaster determine what happens when they walk in. Most of the Events in this adventure include a **Complication**, which is an optional subplot that may be added at the gamemaster's discretion to make things even more interesting.

Following the Episodes is a section called **End Game**, which suggests how to award AP and lists ideas for ongoing plot lines based on this adventure.

INTRODUCTION

The year 3053 has been one of transition in the Inner Sphere.

The once-mighty Federated Commonwealth was dealt a devastating blow by the Clan invasion, and the impact of that blow was increased by the unexpected death of Hanse Davion. The Federated Commonwealth was forced into an uneasy alliance with the Draconis Combine. Now, Sun-Tzu Liao has taken up the reins of power in the Capellan Confederation and is forging ties with the Free Worlds League, leaving House Davion in a precarious position indeed.

The legendary New Avalon Institute of Science has been charged to find a technological edge with which the Federated Commonwealth may regain their lost power. Most NAIS personnel have been reassigned to weapons development, and in their study of Clan technological innovations, have taken research in bold new directions. The NAIS team working at the top-secret facility on Hyde has discovered a breakthrough in BattleMech technology that promises to exceed Prince Victor's highest expectations.

Unfortunately, House Davion's salvation is in the hands of a madman.

Unbound is a roleplaying adventure set in the **Battle-Tech** universe of 3053, on the Game World of Solaris VII. The player characters become involved in a struggle for control of a radical new technological development that could change the balance of power in the Inner Sphere.

This adventure is designed for a group of two to six Inner Sphere characters with the means to reach Solaris or who are already on the Game World. The group can be

Research contains information players may uncover in their investigations over the course of the adventure. **Cast of Characters** provides vital information on the key non-player characters the player characters will meet. **Locations** describes in detail settings the player characters will visit more than once during the course of the adventure.

The final section is **New Tech**, a look inside the special-projects division of the New Avalon Institute of Science, which lists experimental devices currently in the prototype stage. Some of these new devices may be made available to the player characters during the course of the adventure, and can become a permanent part of your **MechWarrior** campaign.

Special instructions to the gamemaster are printed in **boldface** type.

MARGIN-OF-SUCCESS TABLES

At times, the gamemaster will use Margin-of-Success Tables to determine how much information the players receive from questioning non-player characters or physically investigating an area. Each margin-of-success table lists different information for different margins of success. Unless otherwise noted, the player should receive all the information for the margin of success he rolled, as well as all the information for lower margins of success. For example, a character achieving a margin of success of 3 would receive the information for that level as well as the information for a margin of success of 1 and 2.

THE STORY SO FAR

"War itself never changes. People fight for a cause. People die for a cause. Only the weapons with which war is waged ever change, and this change is something we call 'progress'."
—*The Bleeding Edge of Technology*, by Misha Auburn, New Avalon Press, 3049

Professor Burke Kale was a respected scientist who had been affiliated with the New Avalon Institute of Science for many years. His ground-breaking work with advanced neurohelmet design earned him the post of Senior Project Developer for the NAIS. The research he headed as senior developer was the foundation for the improved BattleMech cockpit and control systems now used extensively by the Federated Commonwealth.

In 3043, Professor Kale proposed a revolutionary interface system that would do away with neurohelmets completely, providing a direct neural link between a MechWarrior and his BattleMech. Using this new interface, a pilot could maneuver his 'Mech as easily as he moved his own body, greatly improving the speed and accuracy of the myomer's neuromuscular response.

The NAIS investigated Professor Kale's proposal, and concluded that the direct neural interface project, dubbed DNI, was not only insufficiently tested but also very dangerous, because it required human test subjects at all levels of development. Citing the risks involved, Professor Kale's superiors denied his request for funding.

Kale continued his DNI research for two more years using private funding, then arranged to be posted to Dark Mirage, a secret NAIS research facility located on the planet Hyde. His continuing position as senior project developer gave him control over all aspects of the facility, including budget and personnel.

In 3047, Kale proposed an advanced neurohelmet and interface system that would allow a pilot to control almost all BattleMech functions directly through the neurohelmet, by-passing the manual controls that currently represent the state of the art. Called a Virtual Reality Piloting Pod (VRPP), this new technology would also reduce the space required by a traditional cockpit and move the cockpit out of the Mech's head. The center torso section was proposed as the best alternate cockpit location.

As the revised proposal offered fewer of the risks and most of the benefits of Professor Kale's DNI system, the second proposal was approved. The NAIS granted funding for the creation of a prototype BattleMech equipped with the new VRPP control system.

Kale somehow managed to win first chance at recruiting the NAIS graduates of the class of 3048 to his VRPP project, and chose his team carefully, considering applicants' ambition as well as their skills. He knew that eventually he would need to be able to control key members of his team.

Taking care to hide his tracks, Kale slowly began to divert facilities, materials, and funding from the virtual-reality research to support his DNI research. After-hours and behind closed doors, he continued his clandestine project, using the virtual-reality breakthroughs as the basis for his pet project.

The advent of the war with the Clans gave Kale access to the Clan's advanced technology, which led to a breakthrough in the VRPP, and thus the DNI, research. The professor developed a neural network that would allow him to go to prototype with his covert DNI project at the same time the VRPP system would be ready for testing.

Kale began recruiting members of the virtual-reality research team for the DNI project, luring most of them with promises of fame and fortune. Each team member was sworn to secrecy and set to work on an individual component, unaware of the full scope of the project. Kale claimed the secrecy was necessary because of fierce and unscrupulous academic competition.

When the control systems were complete, Professor Kale "appropriated" a BattleMech that another team at Dark Mirage had cobbled together out of salvaged Clan equipment to use in his experiment. Because the 'Mech was a patchwork of various systems and components, it suffered degraded overall mobility and efficiency, but offered instead a terrifying appearance that gave the pilot a psychological advantage, in addition to the DNI advantage. It was into this 'Mech, dubbed *Prometheus*, that the DNI- and VRPP-compatible pod was installed.

Kale had the DNI-link surgically implanted into his own brain. Acting as the guinea pig in this deadly experiment, the professor secretly tested the *Prometheus*. The experience of commanding the incredible power of a BattleMech as if it were his own body proved overwhelming to the renegade scientist, and he suffered serious neurological damage.

He came to believe that he was one with the *Prometheus*, and though the incredible sense of power the interface provided was overwhelming, he had become addicted to it. With paranoia eating away at his sanity, Professor Kale disbanded his research team and continued his experiments alone.

Kale informed his team that the DNI experiment had failed. He ordered them to leave Dark Mirage, and to keep their work with him to themselves. The research team agreed to his demands, well aware that if they revealed the project to NAIS authorities for any reason, their careers would be ruined.

Soon thereafter, the professor filed a report with the NAIS declaring the virtual-reality project an abject failure, and shut down the Dark Mirage facility. This aroused the suspicions of several members of Kale's DNI research team, who had seen firsthand that the VRPP was a success. They contacted one another, and by comparing notes on the research each had done for the professor, began to get a better picture of what really had been going on at Dark Mirage.

The research team returned to the Dark Mirage facility only to find Professor Kale, the *Prometheus* BattleMech, and all of their notes on DNI missing. With the knowledge that they had helped to illegally develop a dangerous new technology that could end up in the hands of an enemy of the Federated Commonwealth, they feared for more than their careers.

The team knew something had to be done, but they didn't know where to turn until one of the team members spotted a holotape of the *Prometheus* fighting a duel on the Game World of Solaris VII.

The professor had chosen Solaris for his sanctuary, knowing it was one of the few places in the Inner Sphere where a unique BattleMech could appear without attracting too much attention. Kale initially fought in the arenas of the Game World in an effort to attract a government that would support his DNI research, but each time he interfaced with the *Prometheus* he became more addicted to the illusion of power that interface provided, and soon lived only for the thrill of combat.

The research team decided that in order to save their career with the NAIS, they must go to Solaris and bring back the renegade scientist, his lethal prototype, and his research notes. The team set out for Solaris VII with two "borrowed" NAIS prototype 'Mechs and several crates of parts and weapons variants.

Once on Solaris, the team quickly discovered that the only way to get to Kale was in the arena, and so, enlisting the help of a freelance stablemaster, they established themselves as a new stable, calling themselves the Seven Deadly Sins. Using their prototype BattleMechs, the Deadly Sins began competing in the arenas to win a confrontation with their former mentor.

PLOT SYNOPSIS

The unique nature of the Deadly Sins' BattleMechs attracts the attention of the Solaris government, which hires the player characters to learn the secret of this new technology. During the course of the adventure, the characters must infiltrate the stable in order to question the Deadly Sins and search the facility, gathering information about the mysterious 'Mechs.

While the player characters conduct their investigation, other powers are also at work. Agents of the Free Worlds League have caught wind of the unknown stable and their seemingly unbeatable BattleMechs. The NAIS finally discovers the disappearance of Professor Kale and his team, and dispatches a Crisis Intervention Team to retrieve the team and the stolen prototype 'Mechs.

As members of the Deadly Sins, the player characters will have to fight duels on behalf of their stable against an independent cooperative who, unbeknownst to them, is backed by the Free Worlds League. The Deadly Sins earn their match with Kale, but they are betrayed by their stablemaster, who provides the professor with enough information about the Deadly Sins' BattleMechs for the madman to defeat his ex-students with ease. The betrayal and subsequent defeat prompts one of the Sins to attempt to murder the stablemaster, and if he succeeds, the player characters are left alone and confused. Their troubles are compounded by the arrival of the NAIS Crisis Intervention Team.

The Crisis Team questions the player characters and the Deadly Sins. The NAIS team quickly decides that their most pressing problem is stopping Professor Kale, not prosecuting the research team for the theft of the prototypes. The two teams decide to work together, and the player characters are sent to arrange a rematch with Professor Kale. The rematch pits one of the player characters, in a VRPP prototype retrofit with prototype weapons systems, against the *Prometheus*. The duel ends with the discovery that Professor Kale has hired a mercenary to pilot the *Prometheus* using a VRPP system.

The climactic confrontation begins when Kale interfaces with his new 'Mech, the *Epimetheus*. This 'Mech is far more powerful than the *Prometheus*, because Kale designed it specifically for use with DNI. No longer inhibited by the makeshift nature of the *Prometheus*, the DNI link becomes too pure, and Kale's mind cannot cope. Kale now believes that he is a god, and slips completely into insanity. He goes on a rampage, carving a wide swath of destruction. Armed with the finest the NAIS can provide, the player characters have to take him out and bring him in before the damage he is doing brings the Game World crashing to a halt.

GETTING STARTED

The player characters join the adventure when a representative of the Solaran government contacts the team and arranges a rendezvous. The exact nature of this first contact is up to the gamemaster, but a mysterious approach would probably work well. Intrigue plays an important part in this adventure, and an obscure beginning will help the players get into the spirit of the adventure.

For example, if the player characters are currently involved in a campaign elsewhere in the Inner Sphere, they could receive a package via special courier or from a close friend or relative containing passage for the characters and their BattleMechs to Solaris, and an ominous note mentioning a vague "job opportunity" but suggesting haste in the face of dire circumstances.

Regardless of the lure, the goal is to get the characters to a rendezvous at a predetermined time and place, for example, the Star League Park at midnight on June 1st under the rain shelter at the statue of SLDF General Amanda Klark. Where and when the rendezvous is scheduled is unimportant, as long as the meeting is held in a relatively quiet but public place.

When the characters arrive, give them a chance to get nervous. Describe an "unnatural quiet" and have them make Perception Tests to see fleeting shadows. When they are thoroughly spooked and ready to take off, a lone figure emerges from the shadows, a small woman with long, black hair wearing a pulse laser pistol under a flowing cape.

This is Loucynda Byrd, vice-chairman of the Solaris Civic Council. She appears to be alone, but several security agents lurk nearby, armed to the teeth and ready to spring out of hiding at the slightest hint of trouble. Drawing a weapon on Loucynda means the player characters will have to complete the interview from a prison cell; attacking her could easily get somebody killed.

After introducing herself, she explains that, while most people have a pretty low opinion of the Council, they are responsible for seeing that the games are run fairly. She describes herself as a troubleshooter. Her job is to keep a lookout for any irregularities in the duels and do what is necessary to end those irregularities. Recently, a series of matches by an up-and-coming stable called the Deadly Sins attracted her attention.

At this point, she produces a portable holovid display and activates it.

Read the following section aloud to the players.

A red and gold *Thunderbolt* squares off against a 'Mech that looks something like a barrel-chested *Crusader*. The *Crusader*-like 'Mech is painted gray and green, with a black-and-gold symbol on its arm composed of a seven and a ceremonial dagger intertwined, like an enamelled tattoo.

Battle is joined, and though the *Thunderbolt*'s pilot fights well, he is no match for the grim *Crusader*. Volley after volley forces the *Thunderbolt* back, but just when it seems the *Crusader* has won, a lucky shot takes off the *Crusader*'s head. The *Thunderbolt* regains its balance and turns away from the decapitated 'Mech, arms raised to the crowd in triumph.

The recording stops, and Loucynda pauses a moment to let the characters think about what they've seen before replaying the head shot as a slow-motion close-up. At this speed and magnification, the recording shows the *Thunderbolt*'s laser connect with the modified *Crusader*'s head. Armor vaporizes as the internal structure melts and flows away, leaving a gaping hole where the humanoid 'Mech's face should be. Moments later, the rest of the head collapses, leaving nothing but a lump on its shoulders.

Loucynda stops the recording again, and asks you to look for the pilot when the laser beam shears through the head. She replays the loop,

but try as you might, you cannot see the doomed pilot. In fact, you can't even make out a cockpit!

With a wry grin, Loucynda tells you that the pilot apparently survived the duel. Though he lost the battle she played for you, he, or someone with the same name, fought for the Deadly Sins the very next day.

Loucynda explains that the Deadly Sins are apparently using a new technology that allows a BattleMech either to be operated by remote control or to have the cockpit located somewhere other than the head. Either way, the stable is costing some of the more prominent residents of Solaris City a lot of money and is interfering with the smooth operation of the games.

Furthermore, she is sure others have also noticed the irregularity, and, like her, have not dismissed the pilot's apparent resurrection as merely a publicity stunt. This new stable must be investigated, and neutralized if necessary, before their advantage upsets the balance of the betting system.

Her network of contacts brought the player characters and their various talents to her attention, and she decided that the team would be ideally suited to infiltrate the Deadly Sins and discover their secrets. The Deadly Sins are looking for new blood, and Loucynda is looking for someone good enough to get a job with the stable, but who is not well known. The new stable seems to be avoiding MechWarriors of note.

She offers the team 40,000 C-Bills plus expenses for the mission. If the players wish to negotiate for more, have one player make an opposed Negotiation (4) Test. The player characters can convince Loucynda to raise her offer by 1,000 C-Bills for every extra point they achieve.

In order to complete the mission they must infiltrate the Deadly Sins, learn as much as they can about the stable and its secrets, and report back to Loucynda. They will receive half their money in advance, and half upon completion of their task. When they agree to her terms, Loucynda will motion one of her protectors forward and produce the team's advance from a small suitcase full of C-Bills.

The same suitcase holds a list of the members of the Deadly Sins and photos of Gordon West, the stablemaster, entering a club in the Black Hills sector called The Pelican. She gives the players a number to call when they have information to report, but warns them that they are not to tell anyone of their involvement with the Solaris government. She ends the conversation by saying "This meeting never happened. I have never seen any of you before in my life," and without another word, slips off into the night.

UNBOUND ◇ *Joining Up*

THE SITUATION

The characters have been hired to investigate the Deadly Sins stable by infiltrating the organization and finding out whatever they can from the inside. This episode consists of three events, which take the characters from their first contact with the stable to their first battle under the Deadly Sins' banner.

The episode begins when the characters make contact with the stablemaster at a night club in the Black Hills and arrange a tryout in an arena just outside of town. If the characters prove themselves worthy, they are hired and taken to the facility run by the stable, where they can begin their investigation

EVENT 1 — MAKING CONTACT

The player characters come to The Pelican looking for members of the Seven Deadly Sins stable. Gordon West, stablemaster for the Sins, is already there, and he is looking for a few good MechWarriors. The research team has decided to hire mercenaries to fight their unimportant challenges so that they remain free to pursue their mission.

The event begins when the characters arrive at The Pelican, which is described in detail in the **Locations** section, p. 58. Describe the club and its patrons as the characters search for the Deadly Sins. If the player characters question any of the patrons or the bartender, they find out that Stablemaster West is in the Blue Room, one of the two bars that flank the main room.

When the characters make their way to the Blue Room, read the following description aloud.

You wade through the throng packing the opulent club to one of the two bars flanking the main room. Straining to make out faces in the flickering light of the holojectors and hoverlights, you search for one familiar face among hundreds.

Patrons ebb and flow around clusters of people, drawn to the prominent citizens of the Black Hills sector. Among the MechWarriors and stablemasters of note, you spot a man you recognize from his picture as Gordon West, leader of the Seven Deadly Sins.

Your quarry is holding court at one of the larger tables in the room, surrounded by a swarm of Mechbunnies, wannabes, and sycophants. Obviously, he has piqued the curiosity of Solaran society, though he seems uncomfortable with the overwhelming attention.

Approaching West through the crowd will be difficult. How the characters accomplish this is determined by the player's creativity and the gamemaster's discretion, but bear in mind that the throng is only a minor obstacle, intended to illustrate the present popularity of the stable and West's discomfort with his newfound fame.

If the characters pay attention to conversations in the crowd, they will overhear chatter about the meteoric rise of the Deadly Sins' stable, the skill of their pilots, and the superiority of their BattleMechs. Questioning the hangers-on will reveal nothing that the group doesn't already know, but could be very entertaining, depending on who they talk to.

CROWD SCENE CHARACTERS

MECHBUNNY

Typical Names: Tina, Candy, Lori, or Sunshine

Description: A sweet young thing, she wears her makeup too thick and her clothes too tight. She is decked out in hastily autographed momentos and the very latest from the arena gift shop, but still manages to be almost as attractive as she pretends.

Personality: A cute and cuddly teenybopper bubbling over with enthusiasm, she is a slap in the face to any woman who wants to be taken seriously. Basically harmless, she lives to bask in the glow of fame.

Quote: "The Deadly Sins? Gee, they're great! I mean, you know what I mean? I mean, Deadly Sins! Wow! They're, like, Deadly, and like, Sins, you know? [giggle] And they're sooooo cute! Can you introduce me?"

SYCOPHANT

Typical Names: Walter, Billy, Edmund, or Larry

Description: Unshaven, unkempt, and disheveled, it is surprising he was allowed in the club. His jacket hangs loosely from his sloping shoulders and is covered in buttons and pins bearing the symbols, trademarks, and logos of hundreds of stables, cooperatives, and arenas, and various sayings and witticisms associated with the Games. His pale features are twisted in an expression of wide-eyed adoration that is even more repulsive than his lack of personal hygiene.

Personality: Having no life of his own, he lives vicariously through the exploits of his favorite MechWarriors. Though he knows very little of value or interest, he repeats his slim store of knowledge over and over again, hoping that someone will be impressed. The problem isn't getting him to talk, it is getting him to stop.

Quote: "Of course I know about the Deadly Sins. I follow ALL the games. I record all the coverage because every channel follows the matches a little differently. These guys are tops. I can tell. It's like the Sampson brothers all over again, except the Sampsons preferred heavier 'Mechs, but still, you can tell. Champions. I have all their fights on disc. You want to come over some time and watch them?"

WANNABE

Typical Names: Hitman, Flatline, Phantom, or Stixx

Description: Dressed like a holovid MechWarrior, the wannabe is everything a real pilot learns to avoid in his first week of training. Sure, he looks good, but the price tags are still on some of his gear.

Personality: If you dress like a MechWarrior and you talk like a MechWarrior, you are a MechWarrior, right? He may actually have some talent, but no experience other than the thousands of hours he has logged on the stripped-down simulator at the arcade.

Quote: "Remember my name. When I join the Seven Deadly Sins, you will hear about me. I have chosen their stable for a reason, and you would be wise to stay out of my way."

When the characters finally reach Gordon West, they find him friendly but businesslike. When the player characters explain that they are interested in joining the stable, West will look relieved and suggest they adjourn to one of the bar's private rooms to discuss the matter.

Once he has some privacy and the group's attention, West tells them that the Sins are looking for a select few MechWarriors, preferably pilots with their own BattleMechs and technical support. He also warns them that he has received quite a few applications.

The initial conversation with the stablemaster is very important. West will interview the player characters claiming to be MechWarriors, asking probing questions that will give him some idea of the applicants' experience and

expertise. Following are some of the questions he will work into the conversation during the course of the interview.

—How long have you been a MechWarrior?
—Where were you trained?
—Have you worked for any of the Houses?
—What kind of 'Mech do you prefer to pilot, and why?
—What was your greatest victory?
—What was your worst defeat, and why did you lose?

If the characters capture the stablemaster's interest, he will tell them that he is impressed, but not convinced. He offers to set up a trial match between their best pilot and another applicant using 'Mechs rigged for nonlethal combat. He points out that the nonlethal 'Mech configurations significantly improve the chances of both pilots and 'Mechs surviving the encounter, but that the stable does not guarantee their safety.

If the characters accept his offer, go directly to Event 2, p. 14, which is their trial by combat.

COMPLICATION: BAR FIGHT

This optional complication involves the Dark Knights, a cooperative backed by the Free Worlds League. One of the cooperative's contacts confirmed that the Deadly Sins are using advanced weaponry of unknown origin and instructed the members of the Dark Knights to learn what they can about this new equipment.

If the Knights can set up a match with the Sins, they will be able to obtain data on their opponents' 'Mechs from their own machines' battlerecorders after the fight, and possibly win salvage rights to some of the new tech. The Deadly Sins, however, are only interested in duels that will bring them closer to Professor Kale, and so have refused the Knights' challenge.

Amil Gar, one of the Knights' best MechWarriors, has decided to take matters into his own hands and force the Deadly Sins to accept his challenge by publicly humiliating their stablemaster. He brought three toughs with him as back-up in case things get out of hand.

After interviewing the player characters, West returns to his table in the bar. As the team begins to make their way out of the bar, they see the Dark Knights approach West, obviously looking for trouble.

Read the following section aloud to the players.

The stablemaster returns to his table and a crowd gathers around him once again. From across the room, you notice a small group of men moving purposefully toward him through the press of people. They stand out in the crowd because they are dressed very plainly in black-and-red outfits, their only ornamentation a horned helmet motif worked repeatedly into their clothes and jewelry.

As the group of men nears the table, the onlookers give way, nervously anticipating some kind of confrontation. Stablemaster West, seemingly unimpressed, swings his legs up onto the table, lights a cigar, and addresses the leader of the delegation, punctuating his words with a puff of smoke.

"I told you gentlemen we weren't interested."

The leader of the delegation from the Dark Knights is an unwholesome-looking brute in his late thirties or early forties, with an ill-conceived beard and a shaved head tattooed with the insignia of the various military units with which he has served. The three men with him are run-of-the-mill toughs.

If the characters have been on Solaris for a while and make a Mental Saving Roll, or if they talk to someone in the crowd, they can learn that the toughs are from the Dark Knights Cooperative, which is considered well-connected and employs some promising new talent.

The player characters will have to decide how they will react to the developing situation. If they just ignore it and leave, go to Event 2, p. 14. If the team moves closer to West's table, they will hear Amil cut loose with a barrage of abuse intended to provoke West into accepting his challenge.

Amil rants and raves, calling West a coward and a "Federat kiss-butt," but West's only reaction is a bemused smirk. If the characters attempt to intervene, Amil will challenge them, telling them to get lost, and West will wave them off.

Amil will eventually lose his temper and take a swing at West, but the stablemaster's bodyguard intercepts the shot and is knocked cold. This happens too quickly for the characters to interfere. The Dark Knights have decided to scrap, and so West gets to his feet to defend himself, turning to the characters with a grin and saying, "I guess I could use a little help." A brawl ensues, pitting the stablemaster and the player characters against Amil and his three thugs.

Everyone involved will fight using Unarmed Combat to try and knock out the other combatants. No one will resort to weapons unless one of the player characters draws first, in which case the Dark Knights open fire with their pistols, and the fight turns ugly fast.

If West and the player characters outnumber the Knights or get the upper hand too quickly, bring in several crowd members to fight on the Knights' side (use the same stats as for the Toughs). Trav, The Pelican's bouncer, will wade in against whichever side is winning in Round 4 or later.

The Dark Knights will give up when it becomes obvious they cannot win. West will surrender for his side if the Knights gain the upper hand. In either case, the stablemaster now has to save face, so he will accept their challenge, a turn of events that delights the audience.

He thanks the player characters for their help, and adds that he hopes they are chosen to join the Deadly Sins, so he can give them the pleasure of defeating Amil in the arena. Of course, the Dark Knights' challenge is a perfect example of why the stable needed freelancers in the first place, but West doesn't tell them that.

AMIL GAR

Attributes: BLD 5 (7+), REF 5 (7+), INT 4 (8+), LRN 4 (8+), CHA 2 (10+)
Characteristics: Athletics 8+, Physical 9+, Mental 10+, Social 12+
Skills: Blade 2 (6+), Gambling 2 (8+), Gunnery/'Mech 4 (5+), Medtech 1 (9+), Piloting/'Mech 3 (6+), Small Arms 2 (7+), Streetwise 3 (9+), Technician/'Mech 2 (8+), Unarmed Combat 2 (6+)
Equipment: Knife (Damage 1D6–1), Pistol (Range 1–2/3–4/5–8; Shots 6; Damage 2D6+3)

CONDITION MONITOR											
WF	CONDITION	SAVE	1	2	3	4	5	6	7	8
1	GOOD	3+	☐	☐	☐	☐	☐	☐	☐	☐
2	FAIR	5+	☐	☐	☐	☐	☐	☐	☐	☐
3	POOR	7+	☐	☐	☐	☐	☐	☐	☐	☐
4	SERIOUS	10+	☐	☐	☐	☐	☐	☐	☐	☐
5	CRITICAL	11+	☐	☐	☐	☐	☐	☐	☐	☐

DARK KNIGHT TOUGHS (3)

Attributes: BLD 4 (8+), REF 4 (8+), INT 4 (8+), LRN 3 (9+), CHA 3 (9+)
Characteristics: Athletics 10+, Physical 10+, Mental 11+, Social 11+
Skills: Blade 1 (9+), Small Arms 1 (9+), Streetwise 1 (10+), Unarmed Combat 1 (9+)
Equipment: Knife (Damage 1D6–1), Hold-Out Pistol (Range 1–2/NA/NA; Damage 1D6+3)

CONDITION MONITOR											
WF	CONDITION	SAVE	1	2	3	4	5	6	7	8
1	GOOD	3+	☐	☐	☐	☐	☐	☐	☐	☐
2	FAIR	5+	☐	☐	☐	☐	☐	☐	☐	☐
3	POOR	7+	☐	☐	☐	☐	☐	☐	☐	☐
4	SERIOUS	10+	☐	☐	☐	☐	☐	☐	☐	☐
5	CRITICAL	11+	☐	☐	☐	☐	☐	☐	☐	☐

Tough #1   "Skinny"

CONDITION MONITOR											
WF	CONDITION	SAVE	1	2	3	4	5	6	7	8
1	GOOD	3+	☐	☐	☐	☐	☐	☐	☐	☐
2	FAIR	5+	☐	☐	☐	☐	☐	☐	☐	☐
3	POOR	7+	☐	☐	☐	☐	☐	☐	☐	☐
4	SERIOUS	10+	☐	☐	☐	☐	☐	☐	☐	☐
5	CRITICAL	11+	☐	☐	☐	☐	☐	☐	☐	☐

Tough #2   "Blackbeard"

CONDITION MONITOR											
WF	CONDITION	SAVE	1	2	3	4	5	6	7	8
1	GOOD	3+	☐	☐	☐	☐	☐	☐	☐	☐
2	FAIR	5+	☐	☐	☐	☐	☐	☐	☐	☐
3	POOR	7+	☐	☐	☐	☐	☐	☐	☐	☐
4	SERIOUS	10+	☐	☐	☐	☐	☐	☐	☐	☐
5	CRITICAL	11+	☐	☐	☐	☐	☐	☐	☐	☐

Tough #3   "Scarface"

TRAV

Attributes: BLD 7 (5+), REF 5 (7+), INT 4 (8+), LRN 4 (8+), CHA 3 (9+)
Characteristics: Athletics 6+, Physical 9+, Mental 10+, Social 11+
Advantages: Extraordinary Attribute (Build), Toughness
Skills: Blade 2 (4+), Gambling 1 (8+), Medtech 2 (8+), Small Arms 2 (7+), Streetwise 2 (9+), Unarmed Combat 3 (3+)

CONDITION MONITOR											
WF	CONDITION	SAVE	1	2	3	4	5	6	7	8
1	GOOD	3+	☐	☐	☐	☐	☐	☐	☐	☐
2	FAIR	5+	☐	☐	☐	☐	☐	☐	☐	☐
3	POOR	7+	☐	☐	☐	☐	☐	☐	☐	☐
4	SERIOUS	10+	☐	☐	☐	☐	☐	☐	☐	☐
5	CRITICAL	11+	☐	☐	☐	☐	☐	☐	☐	☐

The combat can be run using the **BattleTech** rules or the **Solaris VII** dueling rules. Using whichever rules the group has agreed on, run the duel as a straightforward battle. Marcus has a Gunnery/'Mech Base Target Number of 5 and a Piloting/'Mech Base Target Number of 5, which should make him a fairly easy target for the player-character MechWarrior. If the player character is having trouble defeating his opponent, he should be reminded to use his Edge points when the situation looks bad.

Damage is recorded as normal in order to determine who wins the duel, but no actual damage is sustained unless a 'Mech falls or suffers from a hand-to-hand physical attack. Normal damage is also recorded for these kinds of attacks, but the damage should be tracked separately as it does not affect and is not affected by the simulated damage.

When the battle is over, West thanks the loser for his time and offers to hire the victor on the spot. His initial offer is 10 percent of the purse and 500 C-Bills per month.

Negotiations require an Opposed Negotiation Skill Roll against the stablemaster, who has a Negotiation Skill Target Number of 4+. If the negotiating character lacks Negotiation skill, he must make an Untrained Skill Roll against his own Social Characteristic target number.

The Margin of Success determines the final offer. If West achieves more points than the negotiating player character, 10 percent of the purse and 500 C-Bills per month is the final offer. If the negotiating player character has a higher margin of success than West, the offer may be raised by 1 percent or 100 C-Bills per month for every point by which he beat West's roll, to a maximum of 15 percent and/or 1,000 C-Bills per month.

When the negotiations end, West invites the characters back to the stable to meet the rest of the Deadly Sins and get settled into their new quarters, which is Event 3.

COMPLICATION: ENEMY ACTION

In this complication, the MechWarrior competing against the player characters for the position with the Deadly Sins is actually a Free Worlds League SAFE operative with the same mission as the player characters; to infiltrate the stable and find out what is giving the Deadly Sins their edge.

The agent managed to find out where the 'Mechs to be used in the test were being stored, break in to the facility, and tamper with the battle computer in both machines, altering the simulation program to give himself an edge. He modified both 'Mechs so that he would have an advantage no matter which 'Mech was assigned to him.

When the player characters check the BattleMech assigned to their team, have all characters who are looking the 'Mech over make a Technician/'Mech Skill check, adding a +3 penalty. The character making the roll with the highest margin of success discovers that the battle computer has been tampered with.

EVENT 2: PROVING GROUND

The characters arrive at the appointed time for their tryout with the Deadly Sins at a small arena called The Pit, which lies just outside of town near the Black Hills sector. To get the player characters started, describe The Pit, which is detailed in **Locations**, p. 62.

Gordon West is waiting for them, along with Tommy Devon and Lorri Barris. The stablemaster introduces Tommy as the stable's medic and Lorri as one of their MechWarriors. (Descriptions of Tommy and Lorri appear in **Cast of Characters**, p. 49.) Give the player characters some time to interact with the team from the Deadly Sins, but the pair is reserved and evasive, answering all questions as noncommittally as possible.

Soon after the characters arrive, their opponent drives up in a battered jeep. He is a large man for a MechWarrior, muscular and graceful. His blonde hair is tied back in a long ponytail, and his square jaw shows evidence of having been broken at one time.

The stablemaster introduces the newcomer as Peter Marcus, a freelance MechWarrior looking to break into the Solaris circuit. Marcus is a personable fellow who seems thrilled to have been given this chance. As soon as introductions have been made all around, everyone heads inside to prepare for the test. At this point, the characters must decide which of them will represent the group in the duel.

The character chosen for the duel will be shown to the 'Mech bay, where he or she can change into a cooling vest and examine his or her assigned BattleMech. Other members of the team may also examine the 'Mech.

West has arranged for two *Phoenix Hawks* to be rigged with special simulation gear that will allow non-lethal combat. The 'Mechs' battlerecorders will simulate the damage that would be done by the *Phoenix Hawks'* armed weapons, but no actual damage will be sustained by either combatant.

Have all player characters examining the battle computer make a Computer Skill check, adding a +2 penalty. The character making the roll with the highest margin of success is able to determine that the simulation program has been altered somehow, though it seems to be functioning perfectly.

Have all characters who examine the simulation program make a Security Systems Skill check at a +4 penalty. The character making this roll with the highest margin of success figures out that the program has been altered to increase the response time of the simulation if a specific code is entered before battle is joined, effectively giving the MechWarrior with the code a substantial edge over his opponent. Unfortunately, the code for speeding up the simulation can only be deciphered with specialized equipment and hours of work.

The stablemaster is anxious to get the match underway, but if the characters discover the problem with the simulator and point out the tampering, West will insist that the other 'Mech be examined. Naturally, the examination will reveal exactly the same kind of tampering. He will have the simulation program dumped from both computers and reloaded from his master computer, which will eliminate the suspect files from both 'Mechs.

If the subroutine is still in place at the start of the match, the agent will activate it and gain a −2 bonus to his Gunnery and Piloting skills, reducing them to Gunnery/'Mech 3 and Piloting/'Mech 3. If the player characters are very clever, they may be able to connect Marcus to the tampering. Depending on how the team goes about proving their suspicions, revealing the saboteur may well cause him to flee The Pit, using force to escape. Marcus will not hesitate to engage in a firefight to buy himself enough time to get to his jeep.

SAFE AGENT/PETER MARCUS

Attributes: BLD 5 (7+), REF 5 (7+), INT 5 (7+), LRN 5 (7+), CHA 5 (7+)
Characteristics: Athletics 8+, Physical 8+, Mental 8+, Social 8+
Skills: Communications/Conventional 1 (7+), Computers 3 (5+), Gunnery/'Mech 3 (5+), Medtech 1 (9+), Piloting/'Mech 3 (5+), Security Systems 2 (6+), Small Arms 1 (7+), Stealth 2 (6+), Technician/'Mech 2 (6+)
Equipment: Knife (Damage 1D6−1), Laser Pistol (Range 1–3/4–6/7–12; Damage +D6)

CONDITION MONITOR										
WF	CONDITION	SAVE	1	2	3	4	5	6	7	8
1	GOOD	3+	☐	☐	☐	☐	☐	☐	☐	☐
2	FAIR	5+	☐	☐	☐	☐	☐	☐	☐	☐
3	POOR	7+	☐	☐	☐	☐	☐	☐	☐	☐
4	SERIOUS	10+	☐	☐	☐	☐	☐	☐	☐	☐
5	CRITICAL	11+	☐	☐	☐	☐	☐	☐	☐	☐

deduce from the glimpses they snatch. See the **Introduction** for how to use the Margin-of-Success Table.

Margin of Success	Result
0	These BattleMechs appear to be made up of assorted parts from other 'Mechs. Many components appear to have been professionally machined to fit together, and the stable obviously does not have the proper equipment for such precision work.
1–2	The weaponry on these Battle-Mechs is highly advanced. Some of the weapons match reports of those used by the Clans, while others represent the best arms manufactured in the Federated Commonwealth. The overall cost to put together even one of the Deadly Sins' BattleMechs would be incredible, given this type of armament.
3–4	A glimpse at the head assembly of one of the prototype BattleMechs reveals that there is not enough room in the head for a true cockpit. Other access hatches, however, seem to indicate some sort of a small cockpit in the center torso. These 'Mechs are clearly beyond the current technology known to exist in the Inner Sphere.

INSIDE JOB

EVENT 3

Once the players have successfully negotiated to join the Seven Deadly Sins, they will be introduced to the other members of the stable. They are shown to their new quarters, and given a tour of the facilities.

The player characters will not be allowed to roam freely through the stable or look closely at the equipment and 'Mechs. Lorri Barris will inform the player characters that the 'Mechs are protected by a security sensor, and are considered off-limits to new recruits. Player characters who move toward the restricted area will immediately be noticed by one of the senior members of the stable and assigned an escort.

Inspecting the crates of spare parts and other equipment is somewhat easier, as is access to the armaments and ammo storage area. Player characters who successfully gain access to one of these areas and inspect the crates or their contents must make a Perception Skill check at a +2 penalty. If the roll is successful, the characters notice traces of the ID letters NAIS that were overlooked when the crates were repainted.

Because the player characters are now members of the Deadly Sins, they should bring their 'Mechs to the stable for storage and an inspection by Senior Tech Kavin Drek. Any repairs the player characters' 'Mechs require will be taken care of during their first few days with the stable. The Deadly Sins will probably have the replacement parts necessary to complete all repairs.

While direct access to the "guts" of the prototype BattleMechs is not possible, they are worked on once per day, and player characters with Technician/'Mech Skill may make a skill check at +1 to determine if they see anything unusual about the Sins' private 'Mechs. The Margin of Success determines how much the characters

If the player characters ask questions or make comments based on the above observations, the Deadly Sins will continue to be evasive and refuse to acknowledge anything unusual about their equipment.

The team may decide to check the Sins' personal gear when the stable members leave their quarters. The player characters must make an Unopposed Stealth Skill check with no modifiers. (The security system is constantly manned by at least one senior member of the stable.) A successful Stealth Skill check indicates that no one noticed their attempt to investigate the personal gear, or that the search was made without leaving traces of an intrusion. If the team fails their Stealth Skill check, the gamemaster may allow a chance encounter with one of the Sins while the characters are snooping around, or the characters may accidentally leave evidence that they were searching.

Each player character involved in the search should make a Perception Skill check at a penalty of +1 for Difficulty each half hour while searching the private quarters and gear. If the player character fails the Perception Skill check, he has discovered nothing. A successful Perception Skill check means that the players discover a class ring from the New Avalon Institute of Science in one Sins' personal gear.

Allow the characters to search the complex and question the Deadly Sins as they see fit for a day or two. When the group seems to be running out of ideas, go to Episode 2, p. 20. Don't wait until the players get frustrated and start suggesting foolhardy methods of gathering information; this will lead to a premature confrontation between the team and the Seven Deadly Sins.

Getting acquainted with the Deadly Sins will take some time. For the most part, they use West as a buffer to deal with distractions such as the player characters. They spend most of their time working on various private projects and making contacts which they hope will lead to a duel with Kale. It is difficult to get to the Deadly Sins.

Following are typical encounters with the Deadly Sins. If the characters decide to confront one of the Sins, use that character's entry to resolve the resulting encounter. Don't just run down the list from one character to the next. Wait for the player characters to seek out their employers. If they fail to show any interest in doing so, they are not doing their jobs, and will not pick up the clues these encounters provide.

SEVEN DEADLY SINS

LORRI BARRIS

If the team asks to speak with Lorri Barris, read the following.

You find Lorri Barris in the 'Mech bay behind a wall of crates. She is wearing shorts, boots, and an armored vest over a tight black sweater. As you approach, she pulls a hold-out pistol from under her vest and squeezes off an imaginary shot at an errant coffee mug atop a pile of bricks. Belatedly, she notices her audience. She looks flustered as she holsters her weapon and turns to greet you.

Anyone with Small Arms Skill who makes a successful Perception Skill Test at a +1 modifier notices that Ms. Barris was very fast and her technique near perfect. The red dot of her laser-sight showed that she was dead-on. And her holster is slung for both speed and concealment, suggesting professional training of some kind.

Lorri was running through a practice routine she follows daily to hone her martial arts skills, and will be very embarrassed that she was caught unawares, though she will try not to show it. She is terse and evasive with the characters, partly from embarrassment and partly from the secrecy she has sworn to maintain. She will claim to be very busy, but will take enough time to answer a few questions.

A trained deep-cover agent, Lorri is practiced at fielding awkward questions and can do so with ease. She often tries to turn questions back on the questioner, putting her opponent (for that is how she thinks of all outsiders) on the defensive. For example, if asked, "Where did you learn to shoot like that?" she would respond "Good of you to notice. Do you shoot?" This is meant to be infuriating. Most people get frustrated and just give up.

Any interview with Lorri is going to be short and relatively pointless. Talking with Ms. Barris should leave the characters with more questions than answers, thoroughly confused and unwilling to pursue further conversations with her.

THOMAS DEVON AND AVERY HART

If the team asks to speak with Thomas Devon or Avery Hart, read the following.

Tommy Devon and Avery Hart are in a small room near their sleeping quarters. Tommy is taking several stitches out of the taller man's chest. The medic seems amused at Avery's grim anticipation of the discomfort of each tug. As you approach, Tommy pulls the last stitch, wipes the area with an antiseptic swab, and applies a bandage.

Any character with Piloting/'Mech or Gunnery/'Mech skills who makes a Perception Skill Test at a +2 penalty notices that Hart is not a typical MechWarrior. His head has been shaved to allow for better contact with the neurohelmet's sensors, but there is none of the telltale chafing that normally occurs where the sensors are applied. Hart also seems far too tall for most cockpits. His

lanky form would be folded nearly double by most standard 'Mech designs, which would require extensive modification just to fit him comfortably.

Tommy and Avery head to the common room for some coffee, insisting the characters join them. They will discuss whatever topic the characters bring up, but Tommy is adept at steering the conversation away from sensitive areas. The brilliant young surgeon will toy with the player characters, allowing them to believe they are on the brink of a discovery, then changing the subject.

Avery is nearly Tommy's opposite. Enthusiastic and friendly, he is barely capable of the artifice the research team's precarious position demands, let alone social manipulation for the sport of it. For this reason, Avery is seldom left alone, as his comrades know full well that, of all of them, he is most likely to let information slip. If the characters can catch him alone and give him the third degree, he will indeed reveal a clue, mentioning that it is "good to finally be a true MechWarrior." He will immediately realize what he has said, and will extricate himself from the player characters as soon as he can.

KAVIN DREK

If the player characters ask to speak with Kavin Drek, read the following.

You spot the gangling frame of Kavin Drek hunched over one of the worktables that line the walls of the 'Mech bay. He is working on the emitter tube for a small laser. As you approach, you see him switch out some of the optics with an oversized array that seems to be handmade.

A character with Technician/'Mech Skill who makes a successful Perception Skill Test at a +2 penalty can tell that the new array is similar to that used in an extended-range large laser, but has been tooled down for use with a small laser.

Unless one of the player characters uses this observation as an opening conversational gambit, Kavin will not be receptive to idle chitchat. It will be obvious to the most casual observer that he is obsessive about his work, and has all but shut out the world around him.

If someone mentions the similarity of his new array to that of an ER large laser, Drek seems to suddenly come to life. He will compliment the character on his keen sight and tell him that the resemblance is intentional. Kavin will

claim that the ER small laser is his pet project, but he has had very little success so far. This time, he intends to try using the power packs from two small pulse lasers with an alternating capacitor system, but complains that the setup is too bulky.

As long as the characters want to talk about his current project, Drek will babble incessantly, but if conversation turns to other subjects, such as where he learned his craft and what other projects he is working on, he will excuse himself abruptly and return to his work. A player character who makes a Social Saving Roll at a +2 penalty can tell that the man is hiding something. If the player character fails the saving roll, it is easy to mistake his change of heart for a return to his obsessive behavior.

DIANA HUNSAKER

If the player characters ask to speak with Diana Hunsaker, read the following.

Diana is alone at her computer terminal, as usual. Row after row of computations glide past as she stares at the monitor, entering occasional notations on her pocketcomp. She sees your reflection in the glass, but ignores you, and continues with her work.

Any character with Scientific Special Skill who makes a successful Perception Skill Test will notice that Diana is actually multitasking two programs on her terminal and using the combined data in a third program running on the pocketcomp. This is impressive; even more so as she is obviously distracted by the character's presence.

Diana's programs are a complex biochemical analysis of various enzymes used in the DNI solution XA-3. None of this is apparent to the characters, nor would it make any sense to them if she explained what she was doing. Her work is very specialized and appears arcane to the uninitiated. The player characters may understand that she seems to be working on some kind of biochemical analysis.

Ms. Hunsaker is painfully shy, and will give one- or two-word answers to questions whenever possible. Her shyness should be played up so that the characters do not think her rude or antisocial. No matter how the player characters approach her, Diana's prime motivation in dealing with the characters will be getting away from them.

THE SITUATION

As new members of the Deadly Sins stable, the characters are well on their way to fulfilling their contract with the Solaris government. They are also inextricably involved with the stable's many trials and tribulations.

This episode deals with the problems the Deadly Sins, and through them, the player characters, face. The group will deal with a challenge by the Dark Knights Cooperative, betrayal by and the subsequent murder of their stablemaster, and the arrival of the NAIS Crisis Intervention Team.

EVENT 1 CHALLENGE MATCH

Having established themselves as members of the Deadly Sins Stable, the characters know that they may be called to action on behalf of the stable at any time. The call comes sooner than they expect.

The Deadly Sins have been challenged by the Dark Knights Cooperative. At first, the stable ignored the challenge, but the Dark Knights forced the issue in public. This left West little choice but to accept (see the Bar Fight Complication in Episode 1, p. 12, for more on this).

The Dark Knights are covertly backed by SAFE, the Free Worlds League secret service, which hopes to use the cooperative to learn more about the advanced technology used by the Deadly Sins.

Gordon West will meet with the characters to discuss which of them will answer the Dark Knights' challenge. When the characters gather, he addresses them as a group.

Read the following section aloud.

Gordon West strides rapidly back and forth as he delivers what comes across as a diatribe. "We have been challenged by the Dark Knights Cooperative.

"Normally, we would pay no more heed to them than we do to the vermin that infest this great city of ours, but their leader, Amil Gar, was particularly insulting in a particularly public place.

"Ignoring them is no longer an option.

"Neither the Sins nor the Knights rank high enough as stables to warrant a Class 5 match in the House arenas of Solaris City, so we have arranged a Class 3 match at The Pit.

"All you really have to do is show up in order for our stable to save face on this match. As new pilots, you are an unknown quantity on the Solaris circuit, and so just getting into the arena with the Knights will make you look good. And if you look good, we look good.

"It would be nice if you won, and even better if you took Gar down a couple of pegs. We'd like to see him publicly humiliated, but do what you can, and you will be rewarded according to your performance."

The match is scheduled for 1100 hours the next day. The Dark Knights will arrive at the arena three hours early to prep their 'Mechs and make sure everything is in order. The characters can decide when they will go to the arena, but West will suggest they show up at least an hour before the duel.

When the player characters reach The Pit, they are met by a small crowd and several news teams, including one from the Solaris Broadcasting Corporation. As the team heads for the 'Mech bay, they are intercepted by a news crew looking for an interview.

The sportscaster, Paula Slater, is an attractive young woman wearing a red jumpsuit, antiglare goggles, and a compartmented belt, an ensemble in the latest dueling-circuit look. She is eager to meet the unknown warrior who will be going up against the Dark Knights, and would love to get a statement for the record about the upcoming match. If the player character agrees to an interview, Slater will launch into a rapid-fire barrage of questions including the following examples.

—How do you think you will do?

—Have you ever fought on Solaris before?

—Where have you fought?

—What do you think of the Dark Knights?

—Why didn't an established member of the Deadly Sins meet the cooperative's challenge?

—Is there any truth to the rumors about your stable using lostech?

Ms. Slater is an aggressive muckraker who will try to make the MechWarrior look bad. Her intended victim has only to keep his cool, and she will eventually back off and give up. Anyone who can stand up to Paula Slater will end up looking good. (If you are using the Reputation rules from **Solaris VII**, the interview could provide an opportunity for the MechWarrior to improve his rating.)

After the interview, West will lead the characters to the 'Mech bay to make pre-fight preparations. All systems are functioning perfectly, and no problems arise before the match.

The duel should be resolved using either the **BattleTech** rules or the **Solaris VII** dueling system, if available. The MechWarrior fighting for the Dark Knights is a brash lad who calls himself "Hellfire." Hellfire is very aggressive and favors physical attacks, especially charging. He dreams of winning a match with a Death-from-Above attack.

HELLFIRE

Attributes: BLD 4 (8+), REF 6 (6+), INT 5 (7+), LRN 3 (9+), CHA 3 (9+)

Characteristics: Athletics 8+, Physical 7+, Mental 10+, Social 10+

Skills: Gunnery/'Mech 3 (4+), Piloting/'Mech 4 (3+)

The gamemaster should assign a 'Mech to Hellfire based on the 'Mech the player character will be piloting. The Dark Knights' BattleMech should be five or ten tons lighter than the Deadly Sins 'Mech, but at least two of its primary weapons should be upgraded to 3050 (Inner Sphere) technology. Hellfire is known to prefer pulse lasers and short-range missiles.

During the course of the battle, the gamemaster should describe the reactions of the crowd and the maneuvering of the ever-present cameras, especially if this is the MechWarrior's first duel. Providing more than just a bare-bones account of the battles will add excitement and keep all the players involved in the action.

If the player character wins, several news teams will show up to interview him or her, and during the interview, Hellfire will also show up. Like most Dark Knights, the young MechWarrior is a poor loser. He begins to verbally abuse the player character, claiming that his opponent cheated. If the player character loses his or her cool and insults Hellfire, the Knight takes a swing at the MechWarrior, and the situation could easily degenerate into a well-publicized fistfight. The tone of this exchange is similar to the campy post-game interviews that give professional wrestling its distinctive character, and should be played for all it is worth.

When the dust settles and the player characters return to the stable, West will thank them, regardless of how the match turned out. If the player character did well in the match, West will credit the team's account with a 10,000 C-Bill bonus, commenting that "there is more where that came from" if they continue to excel.

CONDITION MONITOR

WF	CONDITION	SAVE	1	2	3	4	5	6	7	8
1	GOOD	3+	☐	☐	☐	☐	☐	☐	☐	☐
2	FAIR	5+	☐	☐	☐	☐	☐	☐	☐	☐
3	POOR	7+	☐	☐	☐	☐	☐	☐	☐	☐
4	SERIOUS	10+	☐	☐	☐	☐	☐	☐	☐	☐
5	CRITICAL	11+	☐	☐	☐	☐	☐	☐	☐	☐

COMPLICATION: MOB POWER

In this optional encounter, the character scheduled to fight in the match against the Dark Knights will receive an invitation for himself and his friends from "a fan" to meet for dinner at The Pelican to discuss "a business proposition." The invitation specifies the exact time and place for the meeting, and requests that the team not discuss the meeting with the rest of the Deadly Sins.

When the characters arrive at the bar, they are directed to a private room, which is empty. A minute or so later, an elderly oriental gentleman and his two massive bodyguards, in stylish suits that are straining at the seams, join them. The bodyguards will give the player characters the once-over, then seat the old man at the head of the table. The old man invites everyone else to sit.

When everyone is seated, read the following.

The old man gazes somberly at the player characters. When his dark eyes have rested on each member of the team in turn, he gives the assembled party a small, controlled smile. He speaks in a quiet, clear voice.

"I bring you greetings from those for whom I speak. We are pleased that you have chosen to hear our words.

"As you are new to the Solaris circuit, I will introduce myself. Those who know the streets call me Yin Pah. You will learn, if you do not already know, that Solaris is run from the streets. That is where the wagers are made that pay the salaries of the Council that believes it is in control.

"We offer you congratulations on your association with the Deadly Sins stable. With luck, success will follow you as closely as it has your employers. May fame and fortune be yours in equal measure.

"The warriors of your stable have done extremely well for a group of relative unknowns. We are confident that you will continue to equal all expectations, despite the rumors and suspicions we have heard against your stable. These do not concern us. We are concerned only that the wagering favors the Deadly Sins. We would like your organization to work with ours.

"We know that you will be fighting the Dark Knights Cooperative at The Pit tomorrow. This is an opportunity from which both our organi-zations could benefit. You are in a position to make a great deal of money, and we hope you have the wisdom to decide what it is that you want and the courage to achieve it."

Yin Pah is highly placed in a prominent Yakuza family on Solaris. He has been sent to convince the player character MechWarrior to throw the match with the Dark Knights. The two bodyguards will ensure that a refusal will not result in Yin Pah's arrest.

The offer is simple. If the MechWarrior loses, he will be paid 50,000 C-Bills, with a bonus of up to 50,000 more for losing convincingly. On the other hand, if the MechWarrior wins the match, Yin Pah can only promise him "the justice of the streets." He warns that others who were extended the same offer and refused were never given a chance to reconsider.

The Yakuza mouthpiece will order and consume a meal during this conversation, and will offer to buy food and drink for the team. His bodyguards will not eat or drink. To build tension in this encounter, ask each player character what he or she will eat and drink. Use the old man's reaction to each team member's answer to hint that those who refuse to share the meal may be insulting the old man, and thus his organization.

The outcome of the meeting will depend upon the character's reaction to the Yakuza's offer. They will probably agree to "think it over" just to get away from the old man's thugs. The meeting could degenerate into a confrontation, in which case Yin Pah's bodyguards will cover his escape.

YIN PAH

Attributes: BLD 3 (9+), REF 5 (7+), INT 6 (6+), LRN 5 (7+), CHA 5 (7+)
Characteristics: Athletics 10+, Physical 8+, Mental 7+, Social 8+
Skills: Administration 2 (5+), Interrogation 2 (6+), Negotiation 3 (5+), Perception 3 (4+), Small Arms 1 (7+), Streetwise 4 (4+), Unarmed Combat 2 (8+)

CONDITION MONITOR

WF	CONDITION	SAVE	1	2	3	4	5	6	7	8
1	GOOD	3+	☐	☐	☐	☐	☐	☐	☐	☐
2	FAIR	5+	☐	☐	☐	☐	☐	☐	☐	☐
3	POOR	7+	☐	☐	☐	☐	☐	☐	☐	☐
4	SERIOUS	10+	☐	☐	☐	☐	☐	☐	☐	☐
5	CRITICAL	11+	☐	☐	☐	☐	☐	☐	☐	☐

BODYGUARDS (2)

Attributes: BLD 6 (6+), REF 5 (7+), INT 4 (8+), LRN 3 (9+), CHA 3 (9+)
Characteristics: Athletics 8+, Physical 9+, Mental 11+, Social 11+
Skills: Blade 2 (6+), Drive 1 (8+), Small Arms 2 (7+), Unarmed Combat 3 (5+)
Equipment: Sternsnacht Pistol (Range 1–2/3–4/5–12; Damage 4D6+2)

CONDITION MONITOR

WF	CONDITION	SAVE	1	2	3	4	5	6	7	8
1	GOOD	3+	☐	☐	☐	☐	☐	☐	☐	☐
2	FAIR	5+	☐	☐	☐	☐	☐	☐	☐	☐
3	POOR	7+	☐	☐	☐	☐	☐	☐	☐	☐
4	SERIOUS	10+	☐	☐	☐	☐	☐	☐	☐	☐
5	CRITICAL	11+	☐	☐	☐	☐	☐	☐	☐	☐

Bodyguard #1

CONDITION MONITOR

WF	CONDITION	SAVE	1	2	3	4	5	6	7	8
1	GOOD	3+	☐	☐	☐	☐	☐	☐	☐	☐
2	FAIR	5+	☐	☐	☐	☐	☐	☐	☐	☐
3	POOR	7+	☐	☐	☐	☐	☐	☐	☐	☐
4	SERIOUS	10+	☐	☐	☐	☐	☐	☐	☐	☐
5	CRITICAL	11+	☐	☐	☐	☐	☐	☐	☐	☐

Bodyguard #2

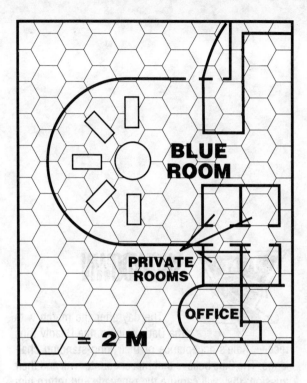

If the player-character MechWarrior loses to the Dark Knight, intentionally or not, a courier will find him as he leaves the stadium and hand over a briefcase containing the promised C-Bills and an origami crane made from the payout stub for a 500,000 C-Bill wager.

If the MechWarrior defeats Hellfire, Yin Pah will hire an assassin to make an attempt on the character's life. This attempt can occur at any point during the adventure, especially when things get confusing, as they might in Event 2: Showdown.

A sniper with a Small Arms Skill of 2+ will take a single shot at a +4 penalty to account for range and concealment. He is using a laser rifle, Damage 4D6+2. If the targeted player character has the Sixth Sense advantage, have him make a Perception Skill Test to sense the attack and perform an Evasion maneuver. If his Perception roll is unsuccessful, he will be unaware of the attack until it has been made.

As the sniper only takes one shot, and that from a concealed position on the roof of a building some distance away, it is extremely unlikely that the player characters will be able to figure out where the shot came from, let alone capture the sniper.

The characters will only know for sure that the shot was an attempted Yakuza hit from a note left for them in a place they will be sure to find it, which says, "The streets can be cruel. Your debt will be collected in full." The Yakuza concept of debt repayment is a subject that can be dealt with in a future adventure if the gamemaster so desires.

SHOWDOWN

The day after the match with the Dark Knights, the Deadly Sins receive Kale's acceptance of their long-standing challenge. The Sins believe that this encounter will end their mission; they will capture the renegade and return him and the experimental equipment to the NAIS, perhaps even keeping their jobs.

The player characters return to the stable from running some errands to find the Deadly Sins in an uproar. A flurry of activity can be seen in the 'Mech bay, where most of the Sins are hard at work on the two prototype BattleMechs. Gordon West intercepts the team with the good news.

He tells them that the stable just received word that they will be dueling a Class 5 contender named Burke Kale in The Factory. West confides that the Sins had set their sights on him from the beginning but will say no more on the subject. In fact, he seems oddly uncomfortable talking about the match, and quickly becomes as evasive as his employers.

The characters can try to take advantage of the excitement of the preparations to get more information for Loucynda Byrd, but the Sins will be more close-mouthed and conspiratorial than ever, and seem single-mindedly committed to getting Avery Hart ready to confront Kale.

When the big day arrives, the player characters are invited to watch the match with West from the stablemaster's skybox. The Factory is crowded, and anticipation and excitement run high. (The description of The Factory in the **Solaris VII Gazetteer** can be used to describe this scene in more detail.) The skybox is a well-appointed booth from which the group can watch the match in privacy and comfort. By the time the team settles in, the start of the match has been announced.

Read the following section aloud.

The two combatants stride into the arena to the cheers of the crowd, taking up positions at either end of a man-made hell programmed to simulate a volcanic wasteland.

The Deadly Sins' 'Mech has been repainted plain white, with serial numbers on most of the major components, making it look like a prototype. Their opponent's 'Mech is a sinister-looking hodgepodge of unidentifiable parts, and resembles nothing so much as a walking salvage heap. Its black-on-black paint scheme gives the hulking monstrosity the bizarre appearance of a twisted shadow.

A flash of light and a piercing buzzer signal the start of the match, spurring both combatants to action. Moving with fluid grace, the two massive machines are expertly maneuvered through the blackened landscape, looking more like giant men than BattleMechs.

West is intent upon the match, but he seems more nervous than anxious. If the player characters ask the stablemaster what he knows about Kale, he replies that no one knows where he came from or what kind of 'Mech he pilots, only that he has made a big name for himself, rising quickly to and through the ranks of the top one hundred MechWarriors.

Any character with Piloting/'Mech Skill who makes a successful Perception Skill Test can tell that the speed and agility displayed by both combatants is remarkable; in fact, it suggests something unusual about the 'Mechs themselves, something beyond the skill of their pilots. This observation is supported by the fact that both 'Mechs move differently from other 'Mechs, displaying a fluidity and coordination of movement usually seen only in humans and animals.

After the characters have had a chance to discuss the combatants, their machines, and the arena in general, read the following.

Battle is joined with a searing laser blast. The two 'Mechs exchange volley after volley as the struggle moves across the broken surface of The Factory. The action moves fast and furiously, the melee a blur that is easier to watch on the replay screens showing slow-motion close-ups of the action.

It quickly becomes obvious that the black *Prometheus* has the upper hand. The Deadly Sins' pilot goes on the defensive, but even that strategy will not save the Sins' 'Mech. Armor melts and metal shreds as Kale's barrage destroys his opponent.

Anyone with Gunnery or Technician/'Mech Skill who makes a successful Perception Skill Test can tell that Kale's 'Mech, the *Prometheus*, is employing Clan weapons systems to systematically sear through the center torso of the Deadly Sins' 'Mech.

In addition, anyone with Piloting/'Mech Skill who makes a successful Perception Skill Test at a +2 penalty will notice that Kale seems to have more than a passing familiarity with the capabilities of the Deadly Sins' Battle-Mech, and he appears to be anticipating every move his opponent makes. Kale forced his enemy off balance in the opening pass of the battle, and pressed the attack constantly, keeping his opponent from recovering. The Deadly Sins pilot does not have a chance.

West seems completely absorbed in the action, staring into the arena with a grim expression on his face. He ignores the player characters' questions and comments, even if they persistently question him about Kale's performance. If the team engages in running commentary about the match among themselves, not bothering the stablemaster with questions, he will suddenly turn on the characters, demanding they allow him to watch his friend die in peace.

When the gamemaster decides that enough time has passed for the match to be nearing its end, read the following.

The *Prometheus* gives the Deadly Sins 'Mech several more minutes of abuse, driving its opponent to its knees. The patchwork *Prometheus* looms over the fallen 'Mech, as if gloating over its defeated enemy. As the Sins' 'Mech struggles to regain its feet, Kale unleashes a laser blast that decimates one of the legs, dropping the 'Mech unceremoniously back to the ground.

The crippled 'Mech raises an arm to fight back, but Kale fires again, disabling the upraised weapon with uncanny accuracy. The defeated 'Mech can no longer struggle, and the *Prometheus* opens up with all its weapons. When the smoke clears, the twisted remains of a chest-mounted cockpit reveal clear evidence of the pilot's death.

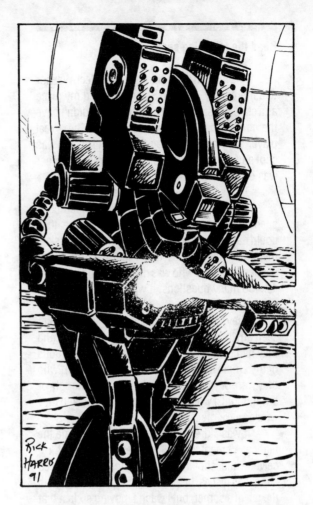

As soon as the match reaches its tragic climax, there is a commotion outside the skybox door. West pales, and asks the team to help him get past the press. If the player characters demand to know why he is acting so strangely, he will promise to answer all their questions as soon as they get him out of the arena.

A clamoring mob of press people outside the box immediately assault the stablemaster with awkward questions that he refuses to answer. The characters will have to push and shove to get West past the media hounds. The reporters in the crowd shout questions and shove cameras in their faces, but the stablemaster just repeats "No comment," over and over, drowning out the player characters if they attempt to reply to the questions.

After several tense minutes, the player characters and West emerge at the exit, where arena security strong-arms them past the mob at the gates. When the group is clear of the arena, the stablemaster will pause to catch his breath. West seems upset by more than just losing the match and a warrior. After a few moments of silence, the stablemaster will try to explain his actions.

Read the following section aloud.

"I have been everything from a MechWarrior to a mercenary. Here on Solaris, I found my place as a stablemaster, but I also found that I didn't have the connections or the ruthlessness to be a real player. My stables came and went, until my rep was shot and my name was poison. I figured my career was over.

"That's when the Sins showed up.

"They found me in the bar where I had been spending every waking hour, and told me they could put my life back together again. I never asked them why they chose me. I just assumed they needed someone who was desperate and wouldn't ask too many questions. It was an offer I couldn't refuse.

"They had their own 'Mechs and gear. I'd never seen anything like what they showed up with, and they had the talent to use it. One of the conditions of my employment was that I never ask them who they were or where they came from. Fair enough, or so I thought. I would keep my mouth shut, and they would make me a lot of money.

"It was a dream come true. They paid me the highest percentage any stablemaster's ever received, and shot through the top one hundred almost as fast as Justin Xiang himself. I was riding the tail of a comet, but I wasn't moving so fast that I didn't see another comet on the horizon.

"Burke Kale showed up on Solaris a week or so before the Deadly Sins with a strange BattleMech that tore through his opponents like he was fighting farmers. By all accounts, the *Prometheus* was unbeatable.

"Right about the time I noticed Kale, my employers informed me that they wanted a match with him. At the time, we were still mucking around in outlying arenas like The Pit, while Kale was already fighting in the city. But they were adamant, and instructed me to arrange matches that would eventually get them to Kale and the *Prometheus*.

"The similarity between the Sins' equipment and Kale's bothered me, but I kept quiet and started working on getting them their match.

"You know most of the rest. You were hired to deal with challenges like the match with the Dark Knights, duels that the Sins knew wouldn't get them any closer to their objective.

"About a week ago, I received an invitation to meet with Kale."

West has become increasingly agitated as he tells his tale. Now he mutters, "I had no choice" and begins to weep. What he is trying to tell the player characters is that Kale forced him to betray the Deadly Sins. What he doesn't know is that Kavin Drek is listening from the nearby shadows. As West's narrative trails off, he will step into the light with a heavy pistol leveled at the stablemaster. He yells "Traitor!" and opens fire.

Drek followed West from the duel, acting on a private suspicion. His sorrow and anger over the betrayal and death of his friend has driven him into an irrational rage, and so the team cannot reason with him.

Only characters with Quickdraw Skill have a chance to stop Kavin from blowing away the stablemaster. Getting off a shot ahead of the murderous tech requires an Opposed Skill Test pitting Drek's Small Arms Skill against the Quickdraw Skill of anyone who tries to get the drop on him.

When Drek appears, Gordon drops to his knees with his face in his hands, waiting to be killed. Drek will fire at the stablemaster unless someone gets in his way or tries to shield West's body, in which case he will hold his fire and try to convince the player characters that West is a traitor and must die.

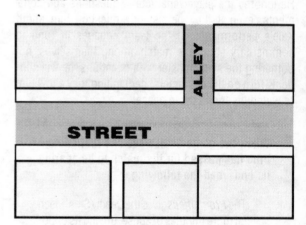

If Drek is subdued, he will eventually calm down. He will tell the characters that he knew the Sins were sold out and that West was the only one in a position to do it. If the stablemaster is still alive, he admits his guilt, adding that Kale threatened to kill him if he didn't reveal the information Kale wanted.

Drek, and West, if he is still alive, eventually decide to return to the arena to take care of Hart's body and retrieve the prototype. They will refuse to allow the team to join them. They consider Hart's death a personal matter, and want to be alone with their friends. The player characters decide to wait for the rest of the Sins at the stable, where Event 3 takes place.

COMPLICATION: AMBUSHED!

SAFE agents have been trailing the Deadly Sins for days. The gamemaster may decide that one or more agents are present when the incident with Drek occurs. SAFE has received orders to capture one of the original Sins, and will see this encounter as a perfect opportunity to do so.

On the turn after Drek opens fire, the agents will attack, targeting the player characters. When the agents attack, Drek is as surprised as anyone, but he will take advantage of the opportunity and try to finish off West. Drek will snap out of his berserker rage in Round 4 and join the characters against the agents.

The agents have Small Arms Skill Target Numbers of 4–6 and carry hand weapons such as pistols. The gamemaster should insert half as many agents as there are player characters, rounding off the number in the characters' favor.

If the player characters take out the SAFE agents, the last agent left will try to escape. If the agents manage to subdue the characters and the stablemaster, they will "liberate" Drek and leave the others lying in the street. If the agents are captured, interrogation will only reveal that they are special agents working for one of the great Houses. They know only the name of their contact, a man they meet at the Stewart Inn.

The player characters will have time to ask only a few questions before twice as many agents show up to retrieve their captured comrades. These agents are armed with laser rifles and are wearing armored bodysuits. They will suggest the characters surrender their captives,

implying that more agents wait nearby. A firefight with the SAFE agents is hopeless. If the team resists with force, the SAFE agents rough them up, and the player characters end up surrendering anyway. The SAFE agents will somehow prevent the player characters from following them (tie the team up, knock them out, and so on) and disappear with Drek.

SAFE AGENTS

Attributes: BLD 5 (7+), REF 5 (7+), INT 5 (7+), LRN 4 (8+), CHA 4 (8+)
Characteristics: Athletics 8+, Physical 8+, Mental 9+, Social 9+
Skills: Blade 2 (6+), Drive 1 (8+), Small Arms 2 (7+), Unarmed Combat 3 (5+)
Equipment: Armored Vest, Pistol (Range 1–2/3–4/5–8; Damage 2D6+3), Rifle (Range 1–6/7–15/16–30; Damage 3D6)

CONDITION MONITOR										
WF	CONDITION	SAVE	1	2	3	4	5	6	7	8
1	GOOD	3+	☐	☐	☐	☐	☐	☐	☐	☐
2	FAIR	5+	☐	☐	☐	☐	☐	☐	☐	☐
3	POOR	7+	☐	☐	☐	☐	☐	☐	☐	☐
4	SERIOUS	10+	☐	☐	☐	☐	☐	☐	☐	☐
5	CRITICAL	11+	☐	☐	☐	☐	☐	☐	☐	☐

Agent #1

CONDITION MONITOR										
WF	CONDITION	SAVE	1	2	3	4	5	6	7	8
1	GOOD	3+	☐	☐	☐	☐	☐	☐	☐	☐
2	FAIR	5+	☐	☐	☐	☐	☐	☐	☐	☐
3	POOR	7+	☐	☐	☐	☐	☐	☐	☐	☐
4	SERIOUS	10+	☐	☐	☐	☐	☐	☐	☐	☐
5	CRITICAL	11+	☐	☐	☐	☐	☐	☐	☐	☐

Agent #2

CONDITION MONITOR										
WF	CONDITION	SAVE	1	2	3	4	5	6	7	8
1	GOOD	3+	☐	☐	☐	☐	☐	☐	☐	☐
2	FAIR	5+	☐	☐	☐	☐	☐	☐	☐	☐
3	POOR	7+	☐	☐	☐	☐	☐	☐	☐	☐
4	SERIOUS	10+	☐	☐	☐	☐	☐	☐	☐	☐
5	CRITICAL	11+	☐	☐	☐	☐	☐	☐	☐	☐

Agent #3

to cooperate, they are still forced to work toward their own goals, at a disadvantage, and NAISCIT will eventually get to the truth without the stable's help, as NAISCIT is monitoring the stable by remote surveillance equipment concealed in the dark corners of the warehouse. The player characters discover Tommy Devon at the warehouse. He arrived just ahead of the team, and was just as surprised to find the stable gone. Tommy asks the characters what happened to the stable, obviously expecting an answer. He also wants to know if they have seen Kavin Drek. Tommy Devon saw Drek storm out after West following the match, and fears what the technician might have done.

Devon also asks about Lorri Barris, who vanished during the match, and Diana Hunsaker, who stayed behind at the stable to prepare their gear for transport, anticipating a victory. Tommy seems to be the only stable member left, and that makes him very nervous.

If the player characters examine the warehouse to try to determine what happened, have each player make a Perception Skill Test. On a successful roll, the players will discover that the crates have been covered with an aerosol dust spray and that the cobwebs are actually synthetic. They also find tracks indicating a truck carried the 'Mechs from the stable.

At this point, the characters may be able to convince Tommy to reveal more about the true origins of the Deadly Sins. They must make a Negotiation Skill Test, modified by −1 to a maximum bonus of −4 for each of the following items they mention to Dr. Devon.

—Any reference to the New Avalon Institute of Science
—Any reference to the unique piloting system on their prototype BattleMechs
—Comparisons of Kale's 'Mech to their own
—Any mention of the new tech items the player characters have seen

The margin of success on this skill roll determines how much information Tommy is willing to part with, according the the Margin-of-Success Table below.

EVENT 3 — INTERCESSION

When the player characters return to the stable, read the following.

Your team enters the stable. When you activate the lights, everyone gives a collective gasp of surprise. The converted warehouse that serves as your stable has reverted back to a warehouse. All of the BattleMechs and equipment are gone, and in their place are several dust-covered crates that look as if they had been there, undisturbed, for months. The living quarters are stripped of gear as well, and have returned to their original condition, right down to the cobwebs in the corners.

When the characters return to the Deadly Sins Stable, they are shocked to discover that everything is gone. The NAIS Crisis Intervention Team, led by Major Jerrold, has returned the warehouse to its original state.

The NAISCIT began following the Seven Deadly Sins shortly after the research team's sudden departure from the Dark Mirage base on Hyde. Aware that another intelligence agency was closing in on the research team posing as a stable, they decided to force the stable's relocation to maintain an advantage.

The NAIS Crisis Team knows that Professor Kale also has come to Solaris, but does not know why he fled the Dark Mirage base. They have decided to reveal their presence to the Deadly Sins in the hope that the research team will surrender the information they require to complete their investigation. If the research team refuses

Margin of Success	Result
1	Tommy admits that Dr. Kale and the Deadly Sins were once research associates. The research team came to Solaris, naming themselves the Seven Deadly Sins, in order to settle an old dispute with their former colleague.
2	Dr. Kale recruited the Seven Deadly Sins as a research team for a secret government research center. He stole something very important, and the research team pooled their resources to try and steal it back.
3	Dr. Kale and the research team worked together at an NAIS facility. Kale stole some new technology they had developed, and the team followed him to Solaris to recover it.
4+	Tommy essentially reveals to the player characters the entire story of how Kale tricked them with his DNI project, and why they pursued him to Solaris to recover it.

Regardless of how much information Tommy is willing to part with about his own affairs, he will inform the players that the stable's disappearance is the work of some sort of Federated Commonwealth intelligence unit.

The NAIS agents monitoring the warehouse wait until Tommy finishes his story before moving to take the group in. Two agents will cover the front door and one will cover the back. These agents are competent and well-equipped, and will not make any mistakes. The team leader flashes Dr. Devon a badge, and announces that by their authority as agents of the Federated Commonwealth they are taking the group in for questioning. He adds that, though Solaris VII is technically outside their jurisdiction, the group would be well-advised not to resist.

Tommy is all in favor of surrendering to the agents, and will encourage the player characters to do the same. If the team goes along quietly, they will find a van waiting for them outside with another agent at the wheel. The player characters get in, and are taken uptown to the Sun and Sword Hotel. One of the agents will accompany them inside, cautioning them to say nothing and make no sudden moves.

When the player characters enter the hotel, read the following.

Your escort tells you to wait and steps up to the plush desk of the hotel. Leaning against the marble-inlaid counter, he speaks to the desk manager, who nods and rings for one of the bellmen. He whispers into the young man's ear, and the bellman motions for you to follow him.

Instead of going toward the main elevators, he takes you to a service elevator at the side of the lobby. He motions for you to enter the elevator. When everyone is inside, he presses the Basement button and steps out before the doors close.

The double doors open in the dimly lit basement of the posh hotel. Down the hall you see light pouring out of a door that is open just a crack. You move forward and open the door. Three people dressed in Federated Commonwealth uniforms look up as you enter.

The leader of the team introduces herself as Major Jerrold of the NAIS Crisis Intervention Team. Her team was activated when Professor Kale and most of his research team disappeared from the Dark Mirage base and reappeared on Solaris.

Their mission is to find out why the research team and Professor Kale are on Solaris and to recover both the personnel and their equipment. They decided to step in ahead of the operational plan when they learned that House Marik's SAFE was conducting their own investigation of the research team. NAIS could not risk having the Deadly Sins or their prototype 'Mechs fall into the wrong hands.

The player characters are told to sit down, and Diana Hunsaker is brought in, looking very nervous. The major motions for her to sit also, then tosses Tommy a passcard with a slip of paper clipped to it. Major Jerrold stands at relaxed attention and addresses her audience.

When the major is ready to speak, read the following.

"You were getting sloppy, and people were starting to notice you for more than your unusually meteoric rise to the top," she begins. "We observed a known SAFE operative casing your stable, and decided that it was time to relocate your operation. If not for our intervention, matters might have gotten out of hand.

"You were foolish to believe you could carry off this little operation without us coming after you. We have had you under observation almost since you left Hyde.

"That passcard will get you in to where your 'Mechs and gear are stored. I would not recommend attempting to leave Solaris VII. I am sure you are aware of how efficient our organization is, and so you must know that any attempt to flee now would be fruitless.

"We don't know the full story behind this operation yet, but it is only a matter of time. If you want to tell me what's going on, I'm willing to listen. Coming clean here and now could make things easier on all of you."

Tommy will immediately launch into the entire tale of the virtual reality project on Hyde, the covert DNI experiment, and Professor Kale's ultimate betrayal. Diana adds that she believes Kale to be suffering from a severe mental strain as a result of his DNI links to the *Prometheus*. What she observed during his matches in the *Prometheus* indicate that while he is in the BattleMech, his personality borders on the psychopathic. Diana feels that he is on the edge of insanity.

When Diana finishes her evaluation, Major Jerrold turns to the player characters and asks who they are, and

why they have joined the Deadly Sins. If the players tell the truth, that they are working for the Solaris Council investigating the apparently new technology the Deadly Sins are using, the gamemaster should make a Perception Skill Test for the major. On a successful roll, she will believe their story.

If they lie or attempt to conceal their origins, the gamemaster will make an Opposed Interrogation Skill Test roll for the major against the Social Characteristic Target Number of each player character. If the major does not make a successful roll, she will accept whatever story the player characters provide. If Major Jerrold makes a successful roll, she will know the characters are lying and will make note of it for future reference.

Once the major has heard what the players have to say, she will leave two agents with the group while the NAIS team decides on their next course of action. The gamemaster should make this time as intense as possible for the player characters, letting them torture themselves by wondering what the NAIS team will do to them.

The NAIS team returns a few minutes later with several file folders. Any character who makes a successful Perception Skill Test can see that several of the files appear to contain dossiers on the Deadly Sins and the player characters themselves.

Major Jerrold stacks all but one of the files in plain sight of the group. She opens the other file and passes around photographs of a man she calls Winston Davis meeting with people in a dark corner of the Stewart Inn, located in the Marik-maintained Montenegro sector of Solaris.

The major candidly admits to the group that the NAIS investigation of Professor Kale has run into some difficulties. The NAIS team agrees that the Deadly Sins have hit upon the best approach, using the arenas to meet and defeat Kale in a match, thus recovering him and the *Prometheus*.

The only obstacle to this plan is that Kale is very selective about who he takes on as he climbs to the Top 25. NAIS believes that Kale will only take on a rematch with the Deadly Sins if "Doc" Davis, Kale's Senior (and only) Tech, makes the arrangements. Major Jerrold's team trailed Davis and discovered that he has been selling information on Kale's equipment to a SAFE operative.

NAIS proposes that the Deadly Sins continue their efforts to confront Professor Kale. This time, however, they will approach him through "Doc" Davis, blackmailing Davis with the photos of him at the Stewart Inn. This tactic should coerce Davis to convince Kale to confront the Deadly Sins in a rematch. Because this plan seems to suit everyone's best interests, the Deadly Sins (and the player characters) agree to cooperate. The NAIS team

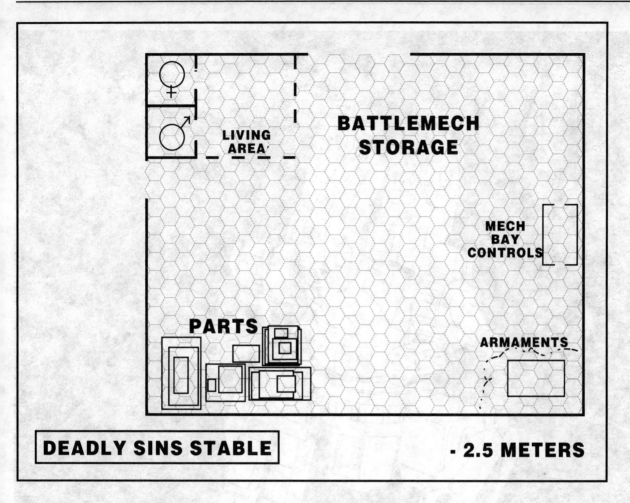

DEADLY SINS STABLE — **2.5 METERS**

transports the Sins to their new stable facility, which is in a better part of the Black Hills sector. Upon their arrival, the group finds their BattleMechs and personal gear in excellent condition. Even their bunks are made up as they left them in the original stable. See the map below for the layout of the new Deadly Sins stable.

DEADLY SINS STABLE MAP KEY

BattleMech Storage

This area holds the entire stable's BattleMechs. The 'Mechs must be arranged back-to-back in this small area, but can still be accessed easily for maintenance and repairs.

Bay Controls

This warehouse features a small, two-person control room for running the crane/winch system built into the ceiling. Security for the warehouse is run through this room as well.

Living Area

The living area is a temporary division of the warehouse space containing five bunk beds. A bathroom facility is located nearby.

Armaments

A makeshift storage facility has been put together for the Deadly Sins' ammunition and missiles. It consists of several heavily armored packing crates covered with three layers of sandbags.

Parts/Gear

All other BattleMech repair gear and parts remain in the original spray-painted storage containers used in the first stable.

If the team checks for electronic bugs or other surveillance, they will find numerous listening devices and at least one miniature camera. Two of the NAIS team operatives will guard the stable at all times, and another two will tail any of the Sins who leave the building. When the team has settled into the new stable, go to the final Episode.

THE SITUATION

The final episode deals with the showdown between the Deadly Sins and Professor Kale. The player characters set up a rematch between the Sins and the renegade, but by the end of the match they realize they have been tricked. Kale hired a MechWarrior to fight for him in the VRPP-controlled *Prometheus*.

During the rematch, the professor returns to his lab to test the *Epimetheus*, thereby stretching his already precarious sanity to the breaking point. Out of control, he goes on a rampage that can only be ended by the characters with the help of the Deadly Sins and their stolen gear.

MATCHMAKER

The player characters' part in the NAISCIT's plan to capture Kale is to set up a rematch between the Deadly Sins and the renegade scientist. The characters travel to the professor's base of operations hoping to blackmail Kale's traitorous tech and right-hand man, Winston Davis, into arranging the match for them.

Before they try to strong-arm Davis, the player characters will have to decide which of them will pose as the stablemaster. It should not be the same character that fought the Dark Knights in the first event of Episode 2, as that character is now publicly known to be a MechWarrior. If the gamemaster wants to sway the decision of which player portrays the stablemaster, he or she can make a recommendation as Major Jerrold. This encounter is an excellent opportunity to focus on one of the non-MechWarrior characters.

Kale's hideout is an old sewage processing station that was converted twenty years ago into a two-Battle-Mech garage. Located in a less-than-desirable area of the Black Hills, the base is isolated and well-protected.

When the team is ready to confront Davis, read the following.

The building itself is impressive. An old sewage-treatment pumping station, this building has almost no windows and is of heavy concrete-and-steel construction. Only one little-used public access leads to this secluded and well-fortified base of operations.

As you approach the station, you see the *Prometheus* standing in one of two berths. On a small gantry near the center torso stands a technician, working on a small sensor. The next bay holds a second 'Mech, covered with tarps to conceal it from casual observation.

Suddenly four bullnecked bodyguards step out of the shadows and stand between your group and the 'Mech bay. They are wearing flak vests and carrying large pulse-laser pistols. They take up positions that make it obvious their orders are to keep people away from the unique BattleMech and its pilot.

The technician lowers the gantry and makes his way toward your group. He sticks a cigarette between his lips and lights it as he interposes himself between you and the bodyguards. The bodyguards back off, as if responding to a higher authority. The tech is Winston "Doc" Davis himself.

Professor Kale has not left his base of operations since he arrived on Solaris, except in the cockpit of the *Prometheus*. He works on the 'Mech almost constantly, incorporating improvements and making sure it is in perfect running condition. Kale is aware of the limitations of his skills, despite the depth of his obsession, and so he hired Winston Davis to help him maintain his 'Mech and manage his stable. Davis is one of the best techs on Solaris VII, and his prices are correspondingly high.

The professor revealed to Doc most of the secrets of the *Prometheus* and its unique pilot interface. Davis has learned even more just from the work he has done on it. Kale is providing him with a wealth of information to pass on to the Free Worlds League, and he intends to take advantage of the situation for as long as possible.

Kale has also become quite paranoid, a symptom of the psychosis induced by the DNI device. Trusting no one other than Davis, he has hired a handful of muscle men to protect him and keep the *Prometheus*' secrets.

If the players characters try to force their way into the 'Mech bay, they find that the bodyguards are skilled with their weapons. Furthermore, they are being paid enough to fight hard to protect Kale and his secrets. Bargaining or reasoning with the guards is of no use. If this encounter degenerates into a shooting match or fistfight, the bodyguards have the following statistics.

KALE'S BODYGUARDS (4)

Attributes: BLD 5 (7+), REF 5 (7+), INT 5 (7+), LRN 3 (9+), CHA 3 (9+)
Characteristics: Athletics 8+, Physical 8+, Mental 10+, Social 10+
Skills: Blade 2 (6+), Drive 2 (6+), Small Arms 3 (5+), Unarmed Combat 3 (5+)
Equipment: Armored Vest, Pulse Laser Pistol (Range 1–2/3–4/5–8; Damage 3D6)

CONDITION MONITOR

WF	CONDITION	SAVE	1	2	3	4	5	6	7	8
1	GOOD	3+	☐	☐	☐	☐	☐	☐	☐	☐
2	FAIR	5+	☐	☐	☐	☐	☐	☐	☐	☐
3	POOR	7+	☐	☐	☐	☐	☐	☐	☐	☐
4	SERIOUS	10+	☐	☐	☐	☐	☐	☐	☐	☐
5	CRITICAL	11+	☐	☐	☐	☐	☐	☐	☐	☐

Bodyguard #1

CONDITION MONITOR

WF	CONDITION	SAVE	1	2	3	4	5	6	7	8
1	GOOD	3+	☐	☐	☐	☐	☐	☐	☐	☐
2	FAIR	5+	☐	☐	☐	☐	☐	☐	☐	☐
3	POOR	7+	☐	☐	☐	☐	☐	☐	☐	☐
4	SERIOUS	10+	☐	☐	☐	☐	☐	☐	☐	☐
5	CRITICAL	11+	☐	☐	☐	☐	☐	☐	☐	☐

Bodyguard #2

CONDITION MONITOR

WF	CONDITION	SAVE	1	2	3	4	5	6	7	8
1	GOOD	3+	☐	☐	☐	☐	☐	☐	☐	☐
2	FAIR	5+	☐	☐	☐	☐	☐	☐	☐	☐
3	POOR	7+	☐	☐	☐	☐	☐	☐	☐	☐
4	SERIOUS	10+	☐	☐	☐	☐	☐	☐	☐	☐
5	CRITICAL	11+	☐	☐	☐	☐	☐	☐	☐	☐

Bodyguard #3

CONDITION MONITOR

WF	CONDITION	SAVE	1	2	3	4	5	6	7	8
1	GOOD	3+	☐	☐	☐	☐	☐	☐	☐	☐
2	FAIR	5+	☐	☐	☐	☐	☐	☐	☐	☐
3	POOR	7+	☐	☐	☐	☐	☐	☐	☐	☐
4	SERIOUS	10+	☐	☐	☐	☐	☐	☐	☐	☐
5	CRITICAL	11+	☐	☐	☐	☐	☐	☐	☐	☐

Bodyguard #4

Davis demands to know who the characters are and what they want. This first stage of negotiation should be very tricky, as Doc knows Kale is not interested in another duel with the Sins. Attempting to blackmail him near Kale and the thugs will also make Doc very nervous.

The characters may want to take a more subtle approach, implying to Davis that they know about his connection with SAFE. If they can get this general idea across, he will quickly suggest they meet somewhere else to discuss the matter further, most likely The Pelican. He will be accompanied by two bodyguards whose loyalty is to him rather than Professor Kale. Their stats are the same as for those listed above.

Davis is a coward who will buckle under quickly if the team threatens him with exposing his activities to Kale and other interested parties. Exposure would kill him, literally, and he knows it. If Kale did not get him, House Marik would. If he managed to stay alive, he would be out of a job. Doc is obviously terrified of the professor, and becomes more nervous every time Kale's name is mentioned.

If the player characters try to question Davis about his employer, he will reveal as little information as possible. He does not know that the player characters already know who Kale is and where he comes from. He will also be very secretive about the *Prometheus*. The only topic Davis will discuss freely is his concern for the professor's physical and mental health, as he assumes that no one will want to fight a crazy man in such a powerful machine. Davis describes Kale's obsession with his 'Mech as an addiction that is ravaging the man's body and soul.

Even though he is willing to arrange the fight, Doc will try and talk the characters out of it, pointing to the death of Avery Hart as proof of Kale's murderous intentions. He will try to avoid providing specifics about the *Prometheus*, speaking of it in hushed tones, almost as though it were a living thing that could overhear him.

The only information Davis can tell the player characters that they don't already know is that the professor is working on a new 'Mech, and that he recently hired a MechWarrior. Kale's paranoia has become so acute that even Davis is no longer privy to the professor's plans, and so cannot tell them what that information means.

After the meeting with Davis, it is only a matter of hours until the rematch is confirmed. Go to Event 2, the showdown in Davion Arena.

PROMETHEUS UNCHAINED

The player characters finally come face to face with the *Prometheus*. The stakes are high: Kale and his new-tech BattleMech, and possibly the balance of power in the Inner Sphere. (Not to mention Kale's current ranking of number 14 on the Solaris Top 25.)

One of the player characters will have to face the *Prometheus* in the arena, because when Kale killed Avery Hart in the first match, he killed the Deadly Sins' only MechWarrior. If there is more than one MechWarrior in the group, the gamemaster should encourage the team to send someone other than the character who fought the Dark Knights to the arena.

The Deadly Sins offer their remaining fully-operational prototype BattleMech for the battle, loading it with whatever missile and prototype ammunition rounds the player desires. This battle is far too important for the Sins to hold anything back. In fact, going no-holds-barred is the only way they will have a chance to win.

Allow the characters to familiarize themselves with the new equipment. Describe the equipment in the **New Tech** section they will be allowed to use, and answer any questions they have about the prototype equipment. This should be exciting for the players, so give them a chance to play with their new gear before moving on.

Over the course of the next few days, the Deadly Sins will train any MechWarriors in the group who want to learn in the use of the virtual-reality piloting equipment and the other new tech, using both the fully operational prototype and the 'Mech used in the first match with Kale, which is currently being repaired. Major Jerrold agrees to have the player characters' 'Mechs retrofit with the new tech weaponry, but her team keeps a close eye on these preparations.

On the day of the match, several NAIS team members will supervise the transportation of the prototype equipment to the arena. They will also check the 'Mech bay for any "nasty little surprises" and keep watch over the Sins, dressed as technicians and concession vendors. The major warns the player characters to be ready for anything, because Kale is almost certainly insane.

The time for the match finally arrives. The chosen MechWarrior suits up. Tommy Devon tells the warrior to "give it to the bastard for Avery," and the major adds "be very, very careful."

When the MechWarrior is ready, read the following.

Davion Arena.

The crowning glory of technology applied to artificial environments, this is the most popular arena on Solaris VII, both with spectators and warriors. Every MechWarrior who fights here believes he will defeat his opponent. His reputation and standing rest on his victory, but that is all. Today, one man must lose for the sake of the whole Inner Sphere.

That man is Professor Burke Kale. Thief, madman, and a potential threat to a way of life.

A voice rings out across the expanse of the Boreal Reach.

"Come little warrior, little ant to be crushed beneath my feet—come, and face your death. Come, and let me drink your blood in victory."

The 'Mech's external speakers echo the renegade's voice through the cavernous arena. Diana had claimed that the prolonged exposure of Kale's nervous system to the *Prometheus* had warped his mind; now it is clear that she was right.

Unaware of the danger promised by the madman's boast, the crowds packed into the stands go wild at his challenge. They will definitely get their money's worth from this match.

"Face me, and perish like those who dared face me before you!" the voice booms, even louder than before.

Suddenly, from beyond the terrain some ninety meters ahead, the hulking shape of the *Prometheus* comes into view. It is a massive monstrosity of war machinery, bristling with weapons and piloted by a madman.

The game has begun.

Following Kale's bold words at the start of the match, the *Prometheus* will be silent for the rest of the duel. This is because Kale is not in the 'Mech. He has hired a mercenary MechWarrior to fight in the *Prometheus*, who played a prerecorded message.

See **New Tech**, p. 73, for descriptions and stats on the prototype 'Mech and the *Prometheus*.

DAVION ARENA

The Davion Arena is a technological marvel able to simulate a wide range of environments. Indeed, the arena may effectively duplicate many of the special features and conditions described for the other Solaris City arenas or in the **BattleTech Compendium**. Any of the maps produced for **BattleTech** are readily adaptable for this purpose.

MERCENARY MECHWARRIOR

Attributes: BLD 4 (8+), REF 5 (7+), INT 5 (7+), LRN 3 (9+), CHA 3 (9+)
Characteristics: Athletics 9+, Physical 8+, Mental 10+, Social 10+
Skills: Gunnery/'Mech 3 (5+), Piloting/'Mech 4 (5+)

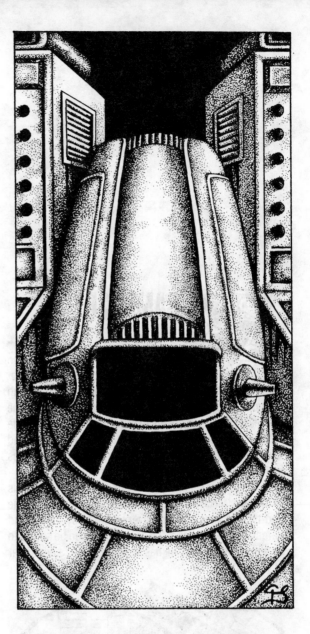

WF	CONDITION	SAVE	1	2	3	4	5	6	7	8
1	GOOD	3+	☐	☐	☐	☐	☐	☐	☐	☐
2	FAIR	5+	☐	☐	☐	☐	☐	☐	☐	☐
3	POOR	7+	☐	☐	☐	☐	☐	☐	☐	☐
4	SERIOUS	10+	☐	☐	☐	☐	☐	☐	☐	☐
5	CRITICAL	11+	☐	☐	☐	☐	☐	☐	☐	☐

CONDITION MONITOR

The match ends when one of the BattleMechs can no longer move or fire. If the *Prometheus* loses the match, a nasty feedback mechanism rigged by Kale will burn out the sensitive VRPP gear Kale supplied for the freelancer, killing the MechWarrior in the process of destroying the new tech.

After the match, more members of the NAIS Crisis Intervention Team arrive, dressed as arena workers. One of them is driving the 'Mech hauler used to transport crippled 'Mechs off the field. As quickly and carefully as possible, the *Prometheus* and the prototype are loaded on the hauler.

Major Jerrold tells the team that the *Prometheus* and the Deadly Sins' remaining prototype 'Mech will be loaded aboard a waiting NAIS DropShip, the *Ogden*, for transport back to Hyde. She thanks the team for recovering the *Prometheus* and thus completing half the Crisis Team's mission, and assures them that the NAIS team can take care of Kale, outlining her plan of action. The NAISCIT will go to Kale's stable to take him into custody. If he is gone, they will recover his paperwork and any remaining equipment. By this time, a crowd of reporters and fight fans has begun to converge on the player characters. The situation becomes chaotic, and Major Jerrold tells the players to get moving; more media exposure will cause too much unwanted publicity.

She asks the team to return to the stable with the Sins until she has a chance to debrief them, which she will do as soon as her team finds Professor Kale.

As Major Jerrold's team approaches Kale's facility, the *Epimetheus* bursts through one of the 'Mech bay walls and starts blasting anything that moves. Diving for cover, they call for back-up. The only back-up available, however, is the Deadly Sins and the player characters, who are on their way back to the stable.

Read the following section aloud.

Your team and the Deadly Sins finally got out of the arena, and are headed back to the stable in the van and car provided by NAIS, when the comm suddenly crackles to life. The voice speaking over the link has not quite controlled his panic.

"Attention base. This is Special Agent Scott of NAISCIT.

"We are under fire at Burke Kale's stable facility. Again, we are under attack.

"It looks like the professor has a new 'Mech and he's gone a little crazy. As far as we can tell, he's killed everyone at his stable and is in the process of laying waste to the surrounding buildings.

"We are pinned down and need back-up.

"You are authorized to commandeer any and all NAIS prototype materiel at your location for use against Kale. Someone has to bring him down, and soon.

"Hurry. I'm not sure how long we can hold out."

EVENT 3 RAMPAGE

While the rematch at Davion Arena was taking place, Professor Kale was performing one last experiment. Even through his increasing paranoia he can guess the real danger of the two teams he knows are out to bring him back to NAIS. He has decided to test the *Epimetheus*, a 'Mech designed specifically for use with the DNI interface. When he plugs in, the link drives him over the edge of insanity.

The rush of sensations provided by the purer signals of the new 'Mech have completed Kale's delusion that he and the machine are one. Overwhelmed by power and paranoia, he knows that the only way he can be safe is to be alone. He believes he has become death, a destroyer of worlds.

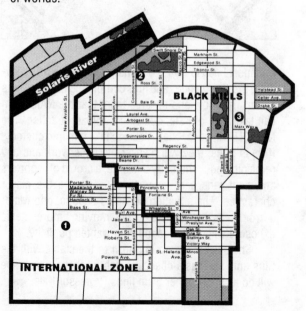

MAP KEY

1 -SOLARIS SPACEPORT

2 -KALE'S LABORATORY

3 -COMSTAR COMPOUND

The Deadly Sins know that their "damage control" needs to begin in earnest now, so they will try to convince the player characters to help. If the team agrees to help take down Kale, the group takes a quick look at a map of Solaris City to figure out the best route back to their stable and the 'Mechs.

The players must drive across the city to reach the stable and the BattleMechs, rolling 1D6 once for each mile they travel through Solaris City. On a result of six they face an encounter that slows them down.

Roll 1D6 on the table below to determine what the team encounters.

Die Roll	Encounter
1	**Traffic Jam**. People leaving the nearby stadium have turned the streets into a parking lot. No traffic is moving. Vehicles are backed up for a kilometer and a half in all directions, with the center of the jam one-half kilometer south of the characters' present position. They can move at one-quarter normal speed around the perimeter of the traffic jam.
2–4	**Police**. The local police force notices the team speeding by and signals them to stop. If the player characters fail to stop, the police initiate a high-speed chase until the team pulls over. They will be heavily ticketed. If they attempt to flee, the police will fire warning shots. If fired upon, the two officers in the car will shoot to kill.
5	**Road Closed for Construction**. The road that the team is traveling suddenly detours up to a kilometer in a direction other than where the characters want to go. The part of the road under construction is nearly impassable. Have the players make several Drive Skill checks if they decide to attempt to navigate the construction work.
6	**Breakdown**. The car develops a mechanical problem of some kind, such as a flat tire. The vehicle is unable to proceed, and the player characters must travel the rest of the distance on foot.

The team must use whatever BattleMechs are in operational condition. Even those badly damaged in previous matches or lacking ammunition will be pressed into the battle. All 'Mechs except the *Prometheus* and the prototype it fought are at the new stable, but Tommy and Diana are the only Deadly Sins left, and so the players will have to pilot the BattleMechs.

The team has the advantage of numerical superiority, even if the damaged prototype 'Mech used in the first fight has not been sufficiently repaired for use.

This battle should be fought using the **BattleTech** rules. Use the blank side of a **BattleTech** map, placing buildings according to the rules below as soon as both sides are within line-of-sight of each other.

Battling in the streets of Solaris City is bound to cause some problems. All buildings are considered Level 1 or higher. For each city block, roll 1D6 for each side of the street to determine how many buildings are on each side of the street. Each building has CF of 1D6 x 10.

Building levels are determined by rolling 2D6 +1 for each building. For example, a roll of 8 indicates that the building is a Level Nine structure (8 + 1), a large obstacle. All buildings have a basement and use the Falling to Basement rules from the **BattleTech Compendium**.

Professor Kale may taunt the player characters throughout the battle. Following are some sample insults to help the gamemaster get started.

—"Come to me, children, and learn what death looks like!"

—"I destroyed those who stood before me in the past, and you also will perish."

—"Behold, I am the destroyer of worlds. The planet trembles under my feet and my hands can crush mountains. You are but ants beneath my heels!"

—"Real warriors would make more of a fight than you. Your petty advances and attacks are nothing to me. I am invincible! I move like the wind and strike like lightning!"

—"I will not grant you escape, tiny warriors. I am your fate—I am death. Come, let me show you the way to hell."

—"You call that an attack? I felt only the bite of a fly. My muscles ache to crush you where you sit. Come closer, and I will snap the head off your pitiful machine and tear out your heart with my teeth."

Professor Kale will not retreat or conceal himself behind any wall sections to block attacks. When possible, the *Epimetheus* will fire at multiple targets at once, even when doing so will put him at a disadvantage. This strategy will help the gamemaster portray Kale's overpowering ego when he is in his metal "body."

When and if Kale is defeated, it will be a shattering blow to his now-fragile ego. Devastated by the damage done to his "body," he will open the torso hatch to the DNI cockpit, climb down, and fall to the ground weeping, slowly curling into the fetal position.

Almost as soon as the battle ends, the player characters find themselves facing more than a dozen police vehicles and several dozen officers. The characters do not have the equipment available to handle this sort of situation.

The police will make the usual demands for surrender, but as long as the player characters remain in their 'Mechs, they outclass the police. Should the characters get out and attempt to negotiate with the authorities, they will be overpowered by the officers and immediately handcuffed.

If any member of the team fires on the Solaris police, the officers will produce two heavy SRM launchers and attack the 'Mech that initiated the attack. Within 3D6 minutes, an additional 4D6 officers equipped with portable SRM launchers will arrive and join in the fight.

If arrested, the player characters will remain in jail for 1D6 hours until the NAIS team's contacts arrange for them to be released to the major's custody.

The player characters can also try to make a beeline for the NAIS DropShip in the 'Mechs, hounded all the way by the local authorities. By the time they reach the ship, however, Major Jerrold's local superiors will have called off the chase.

Once the battle with Kale is over, and the characters have either avoided, or been released by, the authorities, the adventure has ended. See **Endgame**, p. 42, for more on wrapping up the loose ends.

COMPLICATION: BETRAYED

In this complication, Lorri Barris will resurface and steal the *Prometheus* from the *Ogden*. This will take place shortly after the characters arrive back at the stable, as they are getting ready to intercept Professor Kale and the *Epimetheus*. The agents on the *Ogden* will have just enough time to transmit a warning before Barris escapes with the 'Mech.

As the player characters get ready to move out in their 'Mechs, read the following.

As you and the rest of your team settle into your cockpits and try to come up with a plan of action, a voice cuts in on the commlink.

"Say again, this is Team Two. We have a Code Green priority situation.

"Lorri Barris just broke out of here in the *Prometheus*. She is piloting it manually. We believe that she is making for the ComStar Community Center in Solaris City.

"Dispatch all functional BattleMechs to intercept her. Use whatever force is necessary.

"We can't let that tech fall into ComStar's hands. You have to cut her off!"

Lorri Barris is piloting the *Prometheus* using the manual controls (see the Game Notes for the VRPP system in the **New Tech** section, p. 64, for details), and so is moving slowly from the DropShip to the ComStar Center. Major Jerrold will broadcast a warning to all the NAIS 'Mechs, ordering the NAIS team and the player characters not to violate the ComStar Center's grounds. NAIS does not want to risk a major political situation with ComStar.

Lorri will not enter or attack any building. She will not fire at the player characters, but will attempt to flee, moving at the fastest speed possible to get to the Center. She will continue toward the center until she has sustained a total of 25 points of armor damage or any internal damage, at which point she will turn the *Prometheus* and attack the player characters.

Lorri will fight until her BattleMech is unable to move or until she takes a critical hit to the cockpit. In either situation, she will only reluctantly surrender the BattleMech. As soon as she is free of the cockpit, Lorri will attempt to make a break for the ComStar Center on foot.

She will move in and through buildings in an effort to dodge her pursuers. Player characters must make a successful Perception Skill check to be able to spot her in the crowd when she leaves a building they watched her enter.

Firing on the ComStar Community Center or Relay Station is strictly forbidden. ComStar's authority is still strong in 3053, and its presence still respected in many parts of the Inner Sphere. The NAIS team will go to any lengths to make sure that no damage is done to or on ComStar grounds, even if it means allowing Lorri Barris to escape.

END GAME

The gamemaster should refer to this section upon completion of the entire adventure.

AWARDING ADVENTURE POINTS

This adventure offers a great deal of monetary reward, but it also offers the characters a chance to earn adventure points. The number of adventure points awarded is determined by how successful or unsuccessful the player characters are at accomplishing various parts of their mission. (see "Awarding AP", p. 50, **MechWarrior, Second Edition**.)

The group's success determines the extent to which NAIS attempts to cover up the potential scandal and provide assistance to the player characters as a reward for keeping silent about Kale and his research.

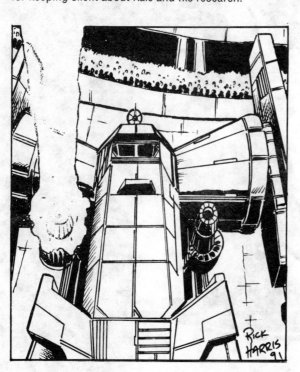

Success	NAIS Assistance/Cooperation
Poor/Fair	"We will overlook your interference because you aided us, but beware your steps in future, because we will be watching."
Average/Good	"In return for your silence, we have repaired your 'Mechs. We have also contacted your employer, Loucynda Byrd, and have reached an agreement with her and the group she represents. She will pay you in full—no questions asked."
Excellent/ Remarkable	"In appreciation for your cooperation and silence in this matter, we have repaired your Battle-Mechs and will transport you anywhere in the Federated Commonwealth you wish to go. We have worked out your agreement with Loucynda Byrd, and she has credited your accounts in full. We have added an additional (1D6) x 1,000 C-Bills as a 'bonus' for your aid in this matter."
Incredible	"For your gracious assistance in this matter, we have repaired your 'Mechs and are prepared to transport you anywhere in the Inner Sphere you desire. Your agreement with Loucynda Byrd has been squared away, and she has paid the agreed-upon fees into your accounts. We are providing a bonus of (1D6) x 10,000 C-Bills credit for your cooperation and continuing silence in this matter. We also have drawn up a contract for your team to serve as test pilots for our Dark Mirage base, testing new weapons as we develop them." (This contract provides for a 1,000 C-Bill retainer per MechWarrior/team member per year, with a bonus of (3D6) x 1,000 C-Bills to be paid if the team is called for testing).

If the player characters inquire about the fate of Professor Kale or the original members of the Deadly Sins, they will be told that, despite the setbacks, the VRPP/DNI research continues, and will perhaps some day give the Federated Commonwealth an edge against the Clans. Kale, if he survived his last encounter with the team, is practically catatonic and has been committed to a hospital. Chances are slim that he will ever recover enough to continue his research—a dark omen for the future of the DNI interface.

LOOSE ENDS

The gamemaster may wish to base future adventures on the following unfinished business.

LORRI BARRIS

As the only known ComStar ROM operative to ever penetrate the veil of security of NAIS, Lorri is considered a prize commodity. If not killed, she may try to escape. The NAIS team may call in the player characters for assistance in tracking her down before she can relay her information to her superiors.

SOMETHING LOST

A stray new-tech missile or an unexploded, unusual new autocannon round may fall into the hands of House Marik, Laio, Kurita, or even ComStar. Agents from any one of these governments might try to track down the player characters to learn about the source of these weapons.

WANNABES

While fighting for the Deadly Sins, the MechWarriors may have earned enough of a reputation to make them the goal of some young MechWarrior looking to make a name for him or herself.

GRUDGE

A grudge is a difficult thing to set aside. Perhaps in one of the team's matches on Solaris VII, someone was killed, and the warrior's siblings or other relatives want revenge. If no one died in the matches, perhaps they were permanently crippled and unable to fight any longer, and are seeking revenge themselves.

CORPORATE JOB

The new-tech items used by Professor Kale and the Deadly Sins attracted media attention. The team might be offered a position in research at one of the corporations on Solaris VII. Imagine the surprise of the corporation when it eventually learns that the player characters know nothing about how to build the new tech!

RECRUITMENT

The NAIS Crisis Intervention Team leader, Major Jerrold, may have been so impressed with the skills of the player characters during the recent crisis that she recommends they form a new Crisis Team for NAIS. They could also be offered short-term jobs assisting the Crisis Team they worked with on this adventure. An assignment such as this could open a veritable Pandora's box of adventures for the players.

NOSEY REPORTER

The small amount of media hype caused by the Deadly Sins and Professor Kale could easily catch the attention of a news reporter. This individual might hound the team to learn the true source of their new-tech equipment, claiming to have seen through the cover story planted by NAIS to the truth.

KALE ON THE LOOSE

Professor Kale might one day snap out of his coma. His now hopelessly twisted mind would be bent on obtaining freedom and revenge—at any cost. The team may be the target of his revenge should he escape. Worse yet, he might seek out the enemies of the Federated Commonwealth to give them access to his knowledge. The player characters could be brought in to stop him once again.

RESEARCH

This chapter provides player characters with background information needed for the adventure. The player characters may question NPCs or contact other sources for information about places and people that affect their mission. Each field of inquiry begins with the **Subject** of the information search followed by **Appropriate Contacts**, which provides the people and places where information may be found; the **Modifier**, which is applied to the inquiring player character's Streetwise Skill roll; and the **Margin of Success Table**, which determines what information is available based on the margin of success achieved by the player character.

BACKGROUND ON LOUCYNDA BYRD

Appropriate Contacts (Modifier –1)

Public-Access Computer and News Files, a wide range of street contacts ranging from any business person or shop owner on Solaris VII to bartenders

Margin of Success	Result
1	"Ms. Loucynda Byrd is well-known as one of the few active individuals on the Solaris Council. She enjoys a very public role in her community."
2–3	"Loucynda is not just another cipher on the Solaris Council. She is said to have connections in every sector and every business on the planet."
4+	"Loucynda Byrd is the troubleshooter for the Solaris Council. Anything at all that threatens to upset the balance of power on Solaris, she considers her affair, and she'll use her business and community assets in whatever manner is necessary to maintain the status quo on the Game World."

PROFESSOR BURKE KALE

Appropriate Contacts (Modifier +1)

Other MechWarriors, Game Followers/Fans, Bartenders

Margin of Success	Result
1	"This Kale fellow has made a significant and rapid climb in the rankings. Rumor has it that his BattleMech has been modified with some lostech devices."
2	"Kale is never seen in public outside his BattleMech. He constantly harangues his opponent during a match, and generally holds a very low opinion of his competition."
3	"I hear Kale is a real mental case. Word is that he's a scrawny thing for a warrior, but you'd never guess that from hearing him boast from the cockpit of that 'Mech of his, the *Prometheus*. Well-placed sources say he has access to Clan technology, which is what gives him his edge in fights."
4+	"Kale is a real recluse. One warrior who claims to have seen him said he was feeble and sickly-looking, yet to hear and see him fight, you would swear he is the hottest jock to ever pilot a BattleMech. As for his technology, rumor has it that Kale has some contacts in the upper echelons at the NAIS, who have smuggled him some of the combat gear he uses. One thing is for sure, the *Prometheus* has yet to be beaten."

THE DARK KNIGHTS COOPERATIVE

Appropriate Contacts (Modifier –1)

Other MechWarriors

Margin of Success	Result
1	"The Dark Knights? Yeah, I've heard of them. Word is that they are pretty crafty fighters."
2	"The Dark Knights—they're a nasty bunch. One of their warriors, a kid who calls himself 'Hellfire,' has kicked some major butt in their last few matches. The word on the street talks about cheating, but so far nobody's been able to prove a thing."
3	"The Dark Knights are connected. No one knows to whom, but they get matches they shouldn't be in, and they've been bailed out of jail a couple of times by stiffs in bad suits."
4+	"Word is, the Dark Knights are backed by one of the Great Houses. No one knows which one, and even if they did, they wouldn't be telling, but they've been seen in Montenegro on more than one occasion. Enough said?"

LOUCYNDA BYRD

Appropriate Contacts (Modifier –1)
Any Solaris Citizen, Reporters, Public Officials

Margin of Success	Result
1	"Byrd? Word is that she's a hard-working member of the Solaris Council. She also has her hands in the middle of everything going on this planet."
2	"Loucynda Byrd? Officially, she sits on the Solaris Council. Unofficially, rumors say she has ties to every one of the major governments set up here, not to mention the mob, the Yakuza and every other criminal element."
3	"Loucynda Byrd is one person whom you do not want to cross. She not only holds a seat on the Solaris Council, but it is well known she has connections all over the planet. Every known stable and business does business through her. They call her The Iron Glue, because she's what is holding this planet together."
4+	"You definitely want to stay out of Byrd's way. She is the troubleshooter for the Solaris Council, which means they use her to ferret out anything that might upset their operations. She has ties to everyone and every government, and most say that she is beyond the reach of even the mighty C-Bill. If you're involved with her, the deal must be very important. More than likely somebody is going to end up dead before it's all over and done with."

YAKUZA OF SOLARIS/YIN PAH

Appropriate Contacts (Modifier –1)
Businessmen and Women, Bartenders, Any "Shady" Characters, Police

Margin of Success	Result
1	"The Yakuza are on Solaris VII, that much is known to be true. Yin Pah is simply a minor warlord for this gang."
2	"The Yakuza have a definite interest in affairs on Solaris. They make a great deal of money from the betting. Yin Pah is one of their midlevel 'moderators,' whose job it is to keep the local businessmen in line."
3	"The Yakuza on Solaris VII are definitely tied into a multitude of operations. Chief of these is the betting on the matches in the various arenas. Yin Pah is one of the Yakuza's most powerful warlords on Solaris, and his hands can be seen in almost every aspect of the gambling business."
4	"Most people think the Yakuza on Solaris make all their money on the shady side of gambling. That is a big part of their income, but they also have a direct role in fight-fixing, and deal in the sale of information. Yin Pah is a dangerous warlord, second in power for the Yakuza on Solaris. Crossing him brings swift death."

NAIS ORGANIZATION, BASES, RESEARCH FACILITIES

Appropriate Contacts (Modifier –2)

House Davion Government Officials, Scientists, BattleMech Technicians

Margin of Success	Result
1	"The NAIS centers most of its primary operations on New Avalon. None of the few remote research bases are known to be close to Solaris, and those that do exist are buried in security."
2	"NAIS research centers dot the Inner Sphere, mostly occupying isolated worlds. Rumor has it that one of these research bases is only three jumps from Solaris and is dedicated to weapons research. But now the word is that security recently clamped down on the place. It appears something, or someone, is missing."
3	"The NAIS is said to have an advanced battlefield technology research center on Hyde, which was closed off in the past few weeks. Apparently, some of the personnel are missing, and the NAIS suspects they have been kidnapped."
4+	"You didn't hear this from me, but NAIS allegedly has hidden a base called Dark Mirage on Hyde. Their secret project is supposed to be one of the greatest innovations in BattleTechnology in centuries, going beyond discovering the secrets of Clan tech. One of their projects apparently got out of hand, and now a whole research team has disappeared, taking a lot of their hardware with them."

THE DEADLY SINS

KAVIN DREK

Attributes

BLD	3	(9+)
REF	4	(8+)
INT	6	(6+)
LRN	5	(7+)
CHA	3	(9+)

Characteristics

Athletics	11+
Physical	8+
Mental	7+
Social	9+

Skills

Computer	3	(4+)
Engineering	2	(5+)
Gambling	1	(6+)
Gunnery/'Mech	1	(7+)
Perception	1	(6+)
Piloting/'Mech	1	(7+)
Security Systems	2	(5+)
Small Arms	2	(6+)
Streetwise	2	(7+)
Technician/'Mech	5	(2+)
Tinker	2	(5+)

CONDITION MONITOR

WF	CONDITION	SAVE	1	2	3	4	5	6	7	8
1	GOOD	3+	☐	☐	☐	☐	☐	☐	☐	☐
2	FAIR	5+	☐	☐	☐	☐	☐	☐	☐	☐
3	POOR	7+	☐	☐	☐	☐	☐	☐	☐	☐
4	SERIOUS	10+	☐	☐	☐	☐	☐	☐	☐	☐
5	CRITICAL	11+	☐	☐	☐	☐	☐	☐	☐	☐

PHYSICAL DESCRIPTION

Kavin Drek is a tall, dark-haired, brooding young man. His face is pockmarked with acne scars, and he appears unkempt and disorganized. His clothes are always far too large for him and long out of fashion, but his habitual scowl prevents anyone from criticizing him.

BACKGROUND

Even as a youth, Kavin showed promise as a technician by field-stripping and rebuilding AgroMechs using only hand tools. As he matured, Kavin became interested in the technical aspects of BattleTechnology. The greatest thrill in his young life was his appointment to the New Avalon Institute of Science.

Professor Kale brought Kavin into his fold by promising to let him do the one thing he really loves—work on BattleMechs. He gained Kavin's cooperation by making him part of a team composed of his true peers, playing on the young man's basic feelings of alienation.

The first to figure out that the professor had duped them, Kavin demanded revenge for the deception. He flew into a nearly uncontrollable rage when he discovered how Kale had betrayed him. It was his idea to go to Solaris and stop the renegade scientist, and he has since been obsessed with the capture of his former mentor.

PERSONALITY

In many ways, Kavin is the classic "nerd" or "techno-geek," because his social skills suffered as he worked to perfect his technical expertise.

An obsessive-compulsive, Kavin is driven in everything he does. His brooding demeanor has earned him the nickname "The Prince of Darkness."

Tommy Devon and Avery Hart tease him relentlessly in good-natured affection, and their obvious caring has gone a long way toward softening his disposition. Still, he is an intense young man who needs to learn how to lighten up.

THOMAS "TOMMY" DEVON

Attributes

BLD	3	(9+)
REF	4	(7+)
INT	5	(7+)
LRN	5	(7+)
CH	5	(7+)

Characteristics

Athletics	11+
Physical	9+
Mental	8+
Social	8+

Advantages:
Natural Aptitude (Medtech)
Wealth

Skills

Administration	1	(7+)
Bureaucracy	1	(7+)
Computer	2	(6+)
Medtech	5	(3+)
Perception	1	(7+)
Protocol	2	(6+)
Seduction	1	(7+)

CONDITION MONITOR

WF	CONDITION	SAVE	1	2	3	4	5	6	7	8
1	GOOD	3+	☐	☐	☐	☐	☐	☐	☐	☐
2	FAIR	5+	☐	☐	☐	☐	☐	☐	☐	☐
3	POOR	7+	☐	☐	☐	☐	☐	☐	☐	☐
4	SERIOUS	10+	☐	☐	☐	☐	☐	☐	☐	☐
5	CRITICAL	11+	☐	☐	☐	☐	☐	☐	☐	☐

PHYSICAL DESCRIPTION

Tommy wears his long, blonde hair tied back in a ponytail. He almost always wears his lab smock, even when he is off duty, and it usually covers a shirt blazoned with the logo of some counterculture band. He perpetually sports a day or two of beard and a wide, knowing grin.

BACKGROUND

Thomas Devon was born the fifth son of the Countess Deidre Devon of Hood IV. Thoroughly spoiled as a child, he nonetheless knew he would not inherit the family title, so he dedicated his energies to becoming a surgeon. His excellence earned him the opportunity to study at the New Avalon Institute of Science.

During his five years at the NAIS, he proved a radical nonconformist. He organized student protests on everything from dormitory food to curfew restrictions. On one occasion, he was placed on probation for striking an instructor who berated him in front of the class.

Professor Kale knew that the young doctor would be pleased to work "outside the system," making him an ideal addition to his research team. Kale used Tommy's rebellious nature to manipulate the young man into working on his DNI project.

Dr. Devon performed the surgery to implant Kale's prototype DNI device. The clandestine operation was performed at 2:00 A.M. in an emergency ward officially closed for renovation. While most surgeons would refuse to work under such conditions, Devon was more than happy to participate in the experiment.

PERSONALITY

Doctor Thomas Devon is one of the brightest neurosurgeons to graduate from the NAIS in the past decade. Unfortunately, Tommy believes his talent and intelligence puts him above rules and regulations.

When he discovered how the research team had been fooled by the professor, Tommy's attitude changed abruptly. For the first time in his life he was part of a team. He paid most of the Deadly Sins' expenses out of his family's own accounts—an action it would not have occurred to him to take only weeks before.

LORRI BARRIS

Attributes			Characteristics	
BLD	4	(8+)	Athletics	8+
REF	6	(6+)	Physical	7+
INT	5	(7+)	Mental	8+
LRN	5	(7+)	Social	8+
CHA	5	(7+)		

Skills

Alternate Identity	3	(5+)
Bureaucracy	1	(7+)
Communications/ Conventional	1	(7+)
Communications/HPG	1	(7+)
Computer	3	(5+)
Cryptography	1	(7+)
Engineering	5	(3+)
Gunnery/'Mech	2	(5+)
Medtech	1	(7+)
Perception	2	(6+)
Piloting/'Mech	1	(6+)
Protocol	1	(7+)
Quickdraw	2	(5+)
Security Systems	2	(6+)
Small Arms	3	(4+)
Stealth	1	(6+)
Technician/'Mech	2	(6+)
Unarmed Combat	2	(6+)

CONDITION MONITOR											
WF	CONDITION	SAVE	1	2	3	4	5	6	7	8	
1	GOOD	3+	☐	☐	☐	☐	☐	☐	☐	☐	☐
2	FAIR	5+	☐	☐	☐	☐	☐	☐	☐	☐	☐
3	POOR	7+	☐	☐	☐	☐	☐	☐	☐	☐	☐
4	SERIOUS	10+	☐	☐	☐	☐	☐	☐	☐	☐	☐
5	CRITICAL	11+	☐	☐	☐	☐	☐	☐	☐	☐	☐

PHYSICAL DESCRIPTION

Lorri is a compact young woman with short-cropped black hair and piercing gray-blue eyes. She usually wears a loose-fitting jumpsuit with a black vest, and an old Star League coin as an earring. Her movements are agile and precise, and display an unusual economy of motion.

BACKGROUND

Lorri Barris was an orphan of the War of 3039. A Com Guard rescue team took her off Royal during the raid by the Crescent Hawks Company. Her rescue by ComStar and her subsequent education in a ComStar school changed her life.

Lorri became a deep-cover operative. Reintroduced into the Federated Commonwealth, Lorri became an engineer, specializing in BattleMech design. Her orders were to infiltrate the New Avalon Institute of Science, a mission she completed successfully, graduating in 3050.

Kale recruited Lorri for the VRPP project and his own covert DNI operation solely on the merits of her skill. Of all the members of the research team, he trusted her the most, passing on to her much of his knowledge and his theories concerning the project.

Lorri is operating under a long-standing order that requires her to report to her superiors anything she observes at NAIS that is likely to upset the balance of power in the Inner Sphere. She has remained with the Deadly Sins so long only because she blames herself for Kale's defection and hopes to correct her mistake before reporting in.

PERSONALITY

Lorri is trained to assume whatever personality is necessary in order to gain access to the knowledge ComStar requires. Most of the time, she is passive, simply listening to what others have to say. She adopts the perky attitude her companions assume is her true nature when it suits her purpose to do so.

She is ashamed that Kale was able to fool her so completely. Secretly, she fears that the situation may already be so far out of hand that ComStar will hold her responsible for the results of Kale's experiments. Anxiety has forced her to fall back on her ROM training, making her ruthlessly manipulate her colleagues.

DIANA HUNSAKER

Attributes

BLD	3	(9+)
REF	3	(9+)
INT	4	(8+)
LRN	6	(6+)
CHA	3	(9+)

Characteristics

Athletics	12+
Physical	11+
Mental	8+
Social	11+

Skills

Administration	2	(6+)
Career Skill: Biochemistry	5	(3+)
Computer	3	(5+)
Medtech	4	(4+)
Perception	2	(6+)
Technician/Electronics	3	(5+)

CONDITION MONITOR

WF	CONDITION	SAVE	1	2	3	4	5	6	7	8
1	GOOD	3+	☐	☐	☐	☐	☐	☐	☐	☐
2	FAIR	5+	☐	☐	☐	☐	☐	☐	☐	☐
3	POOR	7+	☐	☐	☐	☐	☐	☐	☐	☐
4	SERIOUS	10+	☐	☐	☐	☐	☐	☐	☐	☐
5	CRITICAL	11+	☐	☐	☐	☐	☐	☐	☐	☐

PHYSICAL DESCRIPTION

Diana is a small woman who hides her face behind thick glasses, and her stocky figure behind layers of heavy clothing. Painfully shy, she is noticeably uncomfortable in the company of strangers.

BACKGROUND

Diana was raised on New Avalon, and graduated from the NAIS in 3050 with honors in the fields of neurology and biochemistry. Diana was nicknamed "The Hermit" for her all-night sessions in the Auburn Library on the NAIS campus.

Many of her professors suggested that Diana could be one of the finest doctors in her field if she could break out of her shell of shyness. Kale took advantage of Diana's meekness, winning her friendship and using it to lure her to Dark Mirage.

She developed XA-3, the chemical compound used to shield the MechWarrior's mind from neural damage when using the DNI interface, a discovery vital to the success of the project.

PERSONALITY

When Diana discovered that she and the other members of the Alpha Research Team had been tricked by Dr. Kale, the timid researcher became a vindictive shrew. She has made uncharacteristically violent suggestions, such as poisoning her former mentor and friend, or gassing him in his cockpit.

Diana has grown a lot since the team arrived on Solaris. She has gotten to know Dr. Devon and Avery Hart, and became especially close to Hart. Relations between her and Lorri Barris are quite cold, however, despite efforts by Barris to the contrary. Diana is uncomfortable around Lorri, though she has no idea why.

CAST OF CHARACTERS

AVERY HART

Attributes

BLD	5	(7+)
REF	5	(7+)
INT	5	(7+)
LRN	5	(7+)
CHA	4	(8+)

Characteristics

Athletics	8+
Physical	8+
Mental	8+
Social	9+

Skills

Computer	3	(5+)
Engineering	4	(4+)
Gunnery/'Mech	4	(4+)
Medtech	1	(7+)
Piloting/'Mech	2	(6+)
Security Systems	2	(7+)
Small Arms	2	(6+)
Technician/'Mech	3	(5+)
Unarmed Combat	1	(7+)

CONDITION MONITOR

WF	CONDITION	SAVE	1	2	3	4	5	6	7	8
1	GOOD	3+	☐	☐	☐	☐	☐	☐	☐	☐
2	FAIR	5+	☐	☐	☐	☐	☐	☐	☐	☐
3	POOR	7+	☐	☐	☐	☐	☐	☐	☐	☐
4	SERIOUS	10+	☐	☐	☐	☐	☐	☐	☐	☐
5	CRITICAL	11+	☐	☐	☐	☐	☐	☐	☐	☐

PHYSICAL DESCRIPTION

Avery is a lanky young man with bright red hair and freckles, gaunt but muscular. Under a long coat with dozens of pockets he affects the pseudomilitary dress of a MechWarrior. His movements are animated but somewhat awkward, a charming combination.

BACKGROUND

Avery Hart was abandoned at an orphanage as a child. As a young boy raised in foster homes, he developed a love of BattleMechs by watching the Games. Much to his disappointment, by the age of 15 he was already too tall to qualify as a pilot, so he channelled his interest into the technical aspects of BattleTechnology and became an engineer, graduating from the NAIS with top honors.

When Dr. Kale was recruiting assistants for his virtual reality project, Avery practically demanded to be included. The development of VRPP technology would make possible a cockpit that would accommodate any size MechWarrior, offering Avery his long-awaited opportunity to pilot a BattleMech.

Avery was stunned when he learned the professor had betrayed the team's trust. When Drek suggested they track Kale to Solaris VII, Avery volunteered to pilot the prototype 'Mechs in the arenas. His first outings proved to himself and the other members of the team that he was born to be a MechWarrior.

PERSONALITY

An outgoing fellow, Avery has managed to maintain a positive outlook on life despite Kale's treachery. Hart is a good man who is willing to give his life to make things right. Unfortunately, he is more than a little naive, which hooked him into Professor Kale's scheme in the first place.

The amiable would-be MechWarrior is easily the most likeable and approachable member of the Deadly Sins, and may befriend one or more of the player characters.

OTHER CHARACTERS

LOUCYNDA BYRD

Attributes

BLD	3	(9+)
REF	5	(8+)
INT	5	(7+)
LRN	5	(7+)
CHA	6	(6+)

Characteristics

Athletics	10+
Physical	9+
Mental	8+
Social	7+

Skills

Administration	2	(6+)
Bureaucracy	4	(3+)
Computer	1	(7+)
Forgery	2	(6+)
Gambling	2	(6+)
Interrogation	1	(6+)
Leadership	3	(4+)
Negotiation	3	(4+)
Perception	2	(6+)
Protocol	3	(4+)
Small Arms	2	(7+)
Streetwise	4	(3+)

CONDITION MONITOR

WF	CONDITION	SAVE	1	2	3	4	5	6	7	8
1	GOOD	3+	☐	☐	☐	☐	☐	☐	☐	☐
2	FAIR	5+	☐	☐	☐	☐	☐	☐	☐	☐
3	POOR	7+	☐	☐	☐	☐	☐	☐	☐	☐
4	SERIOUS	10+	☐	☐	☐	☐	☐	☐	☐	☐
5	CRITICAL	11+	☐	☐	☐	☐	☐	☐	☐	☐

PHYSICAL DESCRIPTION

Loucynda is a handsome woman who looks as though she would be more comfortable in combat gear than the elegant suits her position demands. Her face is framed by waist-length black hair tied back with a small steel ring. She carries an air of authority that commands the attention of all with whom she comes in contact.

BACKGROUND

Loucynda came from an impoverished family, which provided her the drive and incentive to improve her lot in life. Her ambitions have led her to her current status as one of the most influential mover-and-shakers on the Game World.

One of her first jobs was as clerk for one of the members of the Solaris Council. She learned how corrupt the system was on the Game World, and learned the political tools of the trade she needed to gain information and power. Before she reached the age of 20 she was elected to the Council herself, taking the position of her former employer.

Loucynda sees Solaris for what it is, a profit center. Her function on the Solaris Council is to make sure that nothing interferes with that profitability. To this end she has cultivated a wide range of contacts, including representatives from virtually every business and organized crime syndicate on Solaris VII. While her actions and activities are all aboveboard, they often border on illegal.

PERSONALITY

Most members of the Solaris Council fear Loucynda's ambition, and she knows it. She recognizes the Clans as a great threat, not only to her own way of life, but to the whole Inner Sphere, and there are rumors that she has organized the assorted stables/triads/cooperatives into a covert defense force should the Clans ever attempt to seize Solaris. Anyone who could weld such a diverse group into a fighting force is someone to be feared and respected.

WINSTON "DOC" DAVIS

Attributes

BLD	2	(10+)
REF	4	(8+)
INT	4	(8+)
LRN	6	(6+)
CHA	4	(9+)

Characteristics

Athletics	12+
Physical	10+
Mental	8+
Social	10+

Skills

Computer	3	(5+)
Engineering	3	(5+)
Medtech	1	(7+)
Negotiation	2	(8+)
Perception	1	(7+)
Scrounge	3	(8+)
Security Systems	2	(6+)
Small Arms	1	(9+)
Streetwise	3	(7+)
Technician/'Mech	5	(3+)
Tinker	2	(6+)

CONDITION MONITOR

WF	CONDITION	SAVE	1	2	3	4	5	6	7	8
1	GOOD	3+	☐	☐	☐	☐	☐	☐	☐	☐
2	FAIR	5+	☐	☐	☐	☐	☐	☐	☐	☐
3	POOR	7+	☐	☐	☐	☐	☐	☐	☐	☐
4	SERIOUS	10+	☐	☐	☐	☐	☐	☐	☐	☐
5	CRITICAL	11+	☐	☐	☐	☐	☐	☐	☐	☐

PHYSICAL DESCRIPTION

Davis is nearly bald, with just a trace of hair left over each ear. He wears a hearing aid to compensate for damage done to his eardrum earlier in his military career. Now, at the age of 45, Davis has a dour outlook on life and a crafty personality that helps keep him alive.

BACKGROUND

Winston Davis was born on Loric and spent most of his childhood tinkering with anything mechanical—especially BattleMechs. During a stint as a field technician with the 13th Marik Militia he was wounded by an errant artillery barrage from his own forces, resulting in permanent hearing loss in his left ear.

Davis was a highly skilled technician, and after recovering from his injuries, he decided to exploit his skills to make the money he thought he deserved. In 3030 he arrived on Solaris VII and began working for several small stables, quickly developing a reputation for quality work.

His first big break came when he was hired by the now-defunct White Lancers Cooperative. Over the course of several years he became their chief technician, and by 3043, Davis' reputation was so well known that only the wealthiest stables could afford him. Unfortunately, his ego was as powerful as his skills, and he rarely stayed with an employer for more than a year.

Davis' ego and unflagging desire for money have forced him to begin selling information about his employers to the highest bidders. While this information is not generally known, rumors abound that Davis has become nothing more than a low-level informant for House Marik's SAFE.

PERSONALITY

Since Davis went to work for Professor Kale, arrogant avarice has given way to craven cowardice. The technician has never been accused of being a fool, and has figured out that he is working for a dangerous lunatic with strong ties to one of the Great Houses. He is desperately trying to figure a way out of the situation his greed has landed him in, and hopes his Marik allies can provide a solution.

MAJOR NANCY JERROLD

Attributes

BLD	4	(8+)
REF	5	(7+)
INT	5	(7+)
LRN	5	(7+)
CHA	4	(8+)

Characteristics

Athletics	9+
Physical	8+
Mental	8+
Social	9+

Skills

Alternate Identity	4	(4+)
Blade	2	(7+)
Interrogation	2	(7+)
Leadership	4	(5+)
Medtech	1	(7+)
Perception	2	(6+)
Security Systems	1	(7+)
Small Arms	3	(5+)
Stealth	3	(5+)
Survival	3	(5+)
Tactics	4	(4+)
Training	2	(7+)
Unarmed Combat	2	(7+)

CONDITION MONITOR

WF	CONDITION	SAVE	1	2	3	4	5	6	7	8
1	GOOD	3+	☐	☐	☐	☐	☐	☐	☐	☐
2	FAIR	5+	☐	☐	☐	☐	☐	☐	☐	☐
3	POOR	7+	☐	☐	☐	☐	☐	☐	☐	☐
4	SERIOUS	10+	☐	☐	☐	☐	☐	☐	☐	☐
5	CRITICAL	11+	☐	☐	☐	☐	☐	☐	☐	☐

PHYSICAL DESCRIPTION

Though she is in her late thirties, Major Jerrold appears to be much younger at first glance. The burn scars on her left arm, and two thick streaks of gray hair that contrast with her natural black are clues to her age and experience, but her prototype bionic right arm and facial prosthetics are sleek and appear both natural and youthful.

BACKGROUND

Nancy Jerrold was originally a MechWarrior with the 2nd Crucis Lancers during their operations on Exter during the War of 3039. During the Combine's counter-attack, Nancy's company was overwhelmed and she was officially listed as Missing in Action.

In reality, she was captured by ISF operatives who mistakenly believed her to be an MIIO spy, and endured weeks of torture. She escaped their camp, and despite her serious wounds, eventually made her way back to the Federated Commonwealth.

The information she carried about the Combine's forces was so valuable that she was promoted and transferred to the MIIO. Her first contact with the NAIS came when they coordinated the reconstructive surgery to replace her arm and jaw, shattered during torture.

At the war's end she remained with the MIIO, but she is still listed as Missing in Action. In 3046, Major Jerrold was given the opportunity to transfer to the NAIS to establish a Crisis Intervention Team. Her team's actions during the Tucker and Dana Crisis operations set the standard for future Crisis Teams.

PERSONALITY

Major Jerrold prides herself on her team's ability to operate with little to no support. The assignments that she undertakes are always associated with BattleMechs or BattleTechnology, a pattern her superiors believe displays a longing for her past. During the operation known as the Dana Crisis, her left arm was wounded by an ISF operative who was attempting to steal the plans to the modified *Caesar* BattleMech. She wears the dead agent's dragon unit-insignia on a wristband on her scarred arm.

PROFESSOR BURKE KALE

Attributes

BLD	2	(10+)
REF	3	(9+)
INT	7	(5+)
LRN	6	(6+)
CHA	2	(10+)

Characteristics

Athletics	13+
Physical	8+
Mental	5+
Social	9+

Skills

Administration	2	(3+)
Bureaucracy	2	(3+)
CS: Neurology	5	(0+)
Computer	3	(2+)
Engineering	3	(2+)
Gunnery/'Mech	2	(6+)
Medtech	3	(2+)
Perception	2	(3+)
Piloting/'Mech	1	(7+)
Technician/Electronics	4	(1+)
Technician/'Mech	4	(1+)
Tinker	2	(3+)
Training	3	(2+)

CONDITION MONITOR

WF	CONDITION	SAVE	1	2	3	4	5	6	7	8
1	GOOD	3+	☐	☐	☐	☐	☐	☐	☐	☐
2	FAIR	5+	☐	☐	☐	☐	☐	☐	☐	☐
3	POOR	7+	☐	☐	☐	☐	☐	☐	☐	☐
4	SERIOUS	10+	☐	☐	☐	☐	☐	☐	☐	☐
5	CRITICAL	11+	☐	☐	☐	☐	☐	☐	☐	☐

PHYSICAL DESCRIPTION

His body withered by neglect born of obsession, the professor is a pitiful shell of the man he once was. Gaunt and pale, he appears prematurely old. Animation only returns to his face and movements when he talks about the DNI project, but even these brief moments of excitement wrack his frame with hacking coughs that leave him shaking uncontrollably.

BACKGROUND

Burke Kale was a child prodigy who received special education at a very early age. He had received several degrees and had begun teaching to support himself by his mid-teens, and at age sixteen, he received a full scholarship to the NAIS and graduated with high honors.

Upon completing his education, Kale began a series of experiments funded by government grants that established his reputation as an authority on neurology and led to his appointment to the faculty of the NAIS. His groundbreaking research has earned him a place in history, but has also led to his downfall.

PERSONALITY

His perceptions warped by the psychoactive drugs used in the DNI experiment, the professor believes that he and his 'Mech are one. He is convinced that when he is interfaced with his 'Mech, he is indestructible. He goes so far as to refer to the 'Mech as his body and his tech as his doctor.

On the other hand, when outside of his 'Mech, Kale feels exposed and becomes acutely paranoid. He has trouble communicating with anyone but "Doc" Davis and prefers the solitude of his lab to any other environment. Both in and out of his 'Mech, Burke Kale has become an unbalanced madman whose brilliance only makes him more dangerous.

GORDON WEST

Attributes

BLD	4	(8+)
REF	4	(8+)
INT	5	(7+)
LRN	5	(7+)
CHA	5	(7+)

Characteristics

Athletics	10+
Physical	9+
Mental	8+
Social	8+

Skills

Administration	3	(5+)
Bureaucracy	1	(7+)
Drive	2	(7+)
Gambling	1	(7+)
Gunnery/'Mech	3	(6+)
Leadership	2	(6+)
Medtech	1	(7+)
Negotiation	3	(5+)
Perception	2	(6+)
Piloting/'Mech	2	(7+)
Protocol	1	(7+)
Scrounge	2	(6+)
Small Arms	1	(8+)
Streetwise	3	(5+)
Technician/'Mech	1	(7+)

CONDITION MONITOR

WF	CONDITION	SAVE	1	2	3	4	5	6	7	8
1	GOOD	3+	☐	☐	☐	☐	☐	☐	☐	☐
2	FAIR	5+	☐	☐	☐	☐	☐	☐	☐	☐
3	POOR	7+	☐	☐	☐	☐	☐	☐	☐	☐
4	SERIOUS	10+	☐	☐	☐	☐	☐	☐	☐	☐
5	CRITICAL	11+	☐	☐	☐	☐	☐	☐	☐	☐

PHYSICAL DESCRIPTION

Gordon West is an aging MechWarrior with more of a paunch than he would like. A large man with red hair and a red beard, his jolly appearance matches his outgoing nature. The stablemaster usually wears a flight jacket adorned with the insignia of the various units, stables, cooperatives, and warriors with which he has been associated over the years. It is an impressive collection.

BACKGROUND

West was a mercenary MechWarrior for a time, but his independent nature made a military career unbearable. He tried his hand at the Games. Lacking the skill to be a real contender in a 'Mech, he instead tackled the business end of things and found he had a real talent for managing.

Unfortunately, Gordon did not have the edge required to make his way to the top by stepping on his competitors or to fight off the various underworld ele-

ments that wanted a piece of his action. His stables came and went until his reputation was shot.

When the Sins offered to hire him as their stablemaster, he jumped at the chance, despite the mysterious circumstances of his employers' arrival and the unusual terms of his contract.

PERSONALITY

Competitors deride West as spineless, but the truth of the matter is that he is just an easygoing businessman in over his head. He would have done far better as a salesman, but his fate led him down a different path. He is not a coward, but does not have the fearlessness normally associated with MechWarriors nor the ruthlessness possessed by most stablemasters. Simply put, he is a nice guy in a nasty business, and it will probably get him killed.

LOCATIONS

The following locations are expansions to the material in the **Solaris VII** campaign setting and are used more than once during the course of this adventure.

THE PELICAN

This high-class bar caters primarily to MechWarriors and their guests. Stablemasters and brokers often come here to recruit clients. On Tuesday and Thursday fight nights, its doors are closed to the general public, and MechWarriors watch the games on closed-circuit trivid.

The nightclub was named for the original proprietor, a MechWarrior named Paul Slater. He earned the nickname Pelican for his skill at hunting opposing 'Mechs in the "water" environments of the arenas. Since its founding, the bar has been bought and sold many times, but has always turned a handsome profit for its owners. It is a perpetually popular night spot and enjoys brisk trade and loyal clientele.

The line of people waiting outside the club to gain entrance often stretches around the block. On busy nights the doormen are instructed to admit only celebrities and regular patrons. More often than not, dozens of disappointed hangers-on are turned away without even a glimpse inside.

Manager Lou Kinsel turns a blind eye to most of what goes on in the club, but draws the line at fights or concealed weapons. A six-man security staff is on hand to keep the peace at all times. The chief bouncer, a huge man named Trav, boasts that he defeated a Smoke Jaguar Elemental in hand-to-hand combat on Idlewind, and few men are brave enough to dispute his claim.

THE PELICAN MAP KEY

Blue Room/Green Room

Flanking the main room of the club are two seating areas which offer food and drink to customers who need a break from the hectic activity in the night club proper. The service is slow but friendly, and the food is only mediocre though the prices are high.

A small trivid projector in the center of the room and flatscreen monitors on the walls provide diversions for the diners, who can enjoy rebroadcasts of both recent and famous fights.

Kitchen

Usually presided over by Arnold Willis, a high-strung but capable chef who looks at everyone with an irritating smirk, this is where the meals and other snacks served at The Pelican are prepared. The center of constant, furious activity, this relatively small kitchen produces more food per hour than the kitchens of most other restaurants of comparable size.

Employee Lounge

The Pelican has a staff of anywhere from fifteen to thirty employees on duty at any given time, including a manager, a host or hostess, one to three assistant managers, two doormen, two to six bouncers, two to six bartenders, four to eight waiters and waitresses, and one or two janitors.

The employee lounge provides a place for the employees to get away from the hustle and bustle of their shift. In marked contrast to the rest of The Pelican, this room lacks even a single monitor or projector. It is a quiet room with simple furnishings, designed for rest and relaxation.

Main Room

The main room of The Pelican is impressive. A domed glass roof reveals the sky, and walls lined with monitor screens and projectors simulate environments ranging from various arenas to deep space and underwater scenes.

At the center of the massive club is The Pelican's pride and joy, a trivid projector capable of producing full-size reproductions of arena matches. The projection area is surrounded by a circular bar. Watching a simulation of a fight between two full-scale BattleMechs from less than ten feet away is impressive, to say the least.

From the moment it opens to when the bouncers pour the last patron into a public conveyance, this room is crammed with throngs of people. Just getting from one end of the room to the other can take ten minutes or so. Walking around the club to check out the scene and leaving immediately afterward can take the better part of an hour.

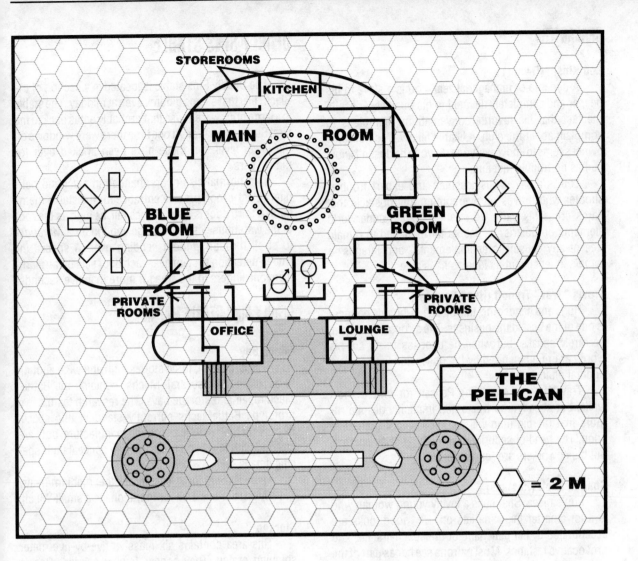

STOREROOMS

KITCHEN

MAIN ROOM

BLUE ROOM

GREEN ROOM

PRIVATE ROOMS

PRIVATE ROOMS

OFFICE

LOUNGE

THE PELICAN

= 2 M

Office

Lou Kinsel practically lives in this suite of rooms that serves as the night club's nerve center. In addition to his office, there is a small conference room, a file room, and a private bath where Lou can shower and change when working double shifts (which he does far too often for his own good health).

The computer terminal on the desk in the office contains all the current employee and financial records in files that can only be accessed by means of a code word. Only Lou and the two managers know the code.

The till is kept in a drop safe built into the floor of the office. A timer unlocks the door three times a day at predetermined intervals, and a manager and at least two armed guards are present each time. The safe is very solid and can withstand continuous laser fire for several minutes before taking damage.

Private Rooms

Many of The Pelican's regular customers desire privacy on occasion while in the club. Eight rooms are available for these "special guests," either for a small fee or as a complementary service, depending on the customer.

As a nod to security, each room is equipped with a camera linked to the security station in the office. Of course, some of the managers can be convinced to forget to turn the camera on, but this often costs more than the room itself.

Storage

These rooms are filled with various supplies that must be restocked every few days. Everything from food to linens can be found here, including dozens of items bearing the club's logo such as napkins, pens, hats, shirts, and ashtrays.

CHARACTERS

Lou Kinsel (Owner)

A dynamo of managerial zeal, Lou is a slave to his beeper and completely devoted to his business, despite the fact that his favorite conversational gambit is to complain about the club. A likable fellow, The Pelican's owner seems to know everyone. Anyone he doesn't know he has no trouble meeting.

Lou is a savvy businessman and expert trouble-shooter who thrives on overcoming any obstacle that dares cross his path. No stranger to the underworld elements on Solaris, he has so far managed to remain free of any "business entanglements" and intends to remain independent as long as he is able.

Travis "Trav" Trunoff (Head Bouncer)

Huge and handsome, this bleached-blonde bouncer is one of the best in the business. The strong, silent type, he rarely speaks, but when he chooses to do so, his words are often inspired by his obsession with ancient oriental philosophy.

Trav has worked at The Pelican for only a short while, but already Lou trusts him implicitly despite rumors that the big man will be "moving on" sometime soon. The head of security is something of an enigma, but his coworkers are fond of him.

Shanna Scott (Hostess)

Lou's niece, Shanna is a lovely young woman who is a lot smarter than she lets on. Her good looks are accentuated by her penchant for unusual hairstyles and provocative fashions. Most patrons see her as part of the scenery, but regular customers know she is a lot more.

Shanna serves as Lou's connection with the Solaris underworld and is largely responsible for keeping the peace. If not for her vigilance and repeated intervention, The Pelican would probably be under syndicate control by now.

Gerald "Jerry" Eastman (Bartender)

Jerry worked at The Pelican long before Lou owned the place. A veteran bartender, the "old man" has worked in most of the hot spots in Solaris City at one time or another during his illustrious career. He trained the other bartenders who now work at The Pelican, and is friend and confidant to most of them.

An expert listener, the head bartender is a very perceptive fellow. Although Lou has more contacts and connections than Jerry, he is far too busy to remember everything he has said and done, and so the regulars turn to Jerry when they want to know what is going down.

DEADLY SINS STABLE

The Deadly Sins stable is located in a section of the Black Hills that seems gloomy even at midday. The stable is a large brick warehouse that probably dates back to the First Succession War. At one time there were windows on the lower level, but these have been bricked over for many years.

Two normal-size doors, banded in steel and definitely blast-proof, provide entrance for the stable members. A third door is three stories tall, as high as the roof of the warehouse itself and large enough for a *Marauder* to stroll through without bending over. A special intruder-detection system near each door sets off an alarm if anyone lingers in the area for more than five seconds.

DEADLY SINS STABLE MAP KEY

'Mech Bay

This large area, three stories high and wide enough to accommodate several 'Mechs, contains the Battle-Mech repair and storage bays. The research team's two prototype BattleMechs currently stand in this space. Because of their unique shape and manufacture, both are covered with tarps and dropcloths to conceal their specific details.

There is room for at least three other medium/heavy BattleMechs in this area, or four if one is a small 'Mech.

Storage

This area contains six massive five-by-five-meter shipping crates. They appear freshly painted. One is open, revealing new myomer bundles and several cockpit-repair components.

Private Quarters

These one-story quarters have been improvised out of the old warehouse offices. Most have half-walls with glass partitions rising to the ceiling. The Deadly Sins painted the windows black and placed two cots in each office space to create makeshift bedrooms. Two more rooms are in the process of being converted.

In the back of this area is a single-stall shower as well as other rest room facilities.

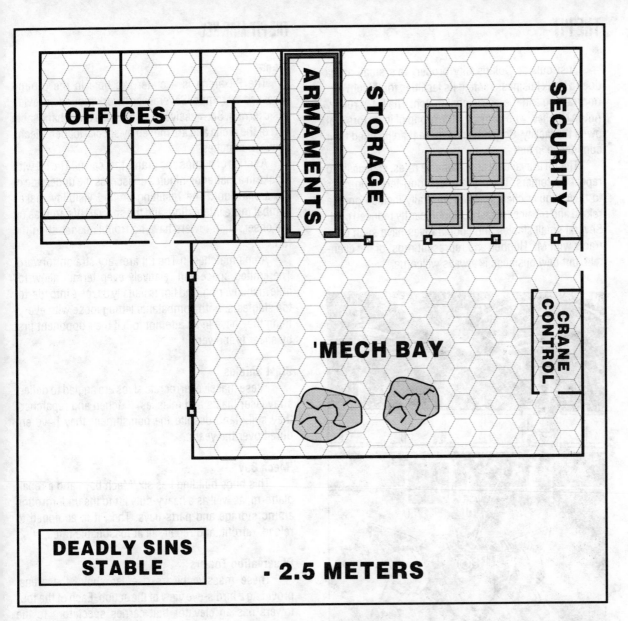

OFFICES

ARMAMENTS

STORAGE

SECURITY

'MECH BAY

CRANE CONTROL

DEADLY SINS STABLE

- 2.5 METERS

Armaments

This brick room looks like a vault and was probably used for security storage decades ago. The Deadly Sins are using it for storing their ammunition and missiles, which are individually wrapped and packed in Federated Commonwealth packing crates. Many of the crates have recently been spray-painted blue in an attempt to hide their true origins.

Security

The Deadly Sins have set up a series of alarms in their stable, and the control systems are hidden in this isolated corner. This system has an audible alarm that sounds if anyone stands within three meters of any of the exterior doors for more than five seconds. Contact sensor alarms have been installed on the Sins' BattleMechs that sound if any unauthorized person touches the machines.

At least one of the Sins watches the security system at all times. When the players join the stable, they will not be rotated to this duty.

Crane Controls

The entire ceiling of the warehouse (not including the area above the offices/living quarters) is laid with grid track. Three mobile cranes run on these tracks, each designed to lift ten tons. This small room is the control center for these cranes.

THE PIT

Just outside Solaris City proper, this small arena does a brisk business renting its facilities for 'MechWarrior training and the occasional match. The Pit is run by Anton Hughes, who works for the group of investors that owns the facility. So far, he has more than justified their confidence in him.

The Pit is available at reasonable rates, especially to repeat customers. The arena offers long-term contracts to their regular clients, which normally include on-site reload and repair services at a significantly reduced cost. Several small stables and cooperatives have such contracts with Mr. Hughes and represent most of his clientele, but new business is always welcome.

THE PIT MAP KEY

Arena

The Pit arena is a crater-like hole in the ground accessed by ramps. Several earthwork mounds provide basic terrain. Six massive pylons are the only changeable part of the arena and are moved by special loader 'Mechs between matches.

A series of pumps and grates that can fill The Pit with smoke in a matter of minutes crisscross the underside of the arena floor. The resulting limited visibility makes combat more interesting, and the special UV cameras on the observation towers have no trouble penetrating the fog.

Arena matches in The Pit are very straightforward. The limited space and relatively even terrain allow for little maneuvering, and fights usually devolve into toe-to-toe slugfests, both combatants letting loose with everything they have in an attempt to fell their opponent first by sheer firepower.

Blast Shields

These massive ferrocrete slabs are angled to deflect stray laser blasts and missiles. Patched and repatched, they still stand despite the punishment they have endured over the years.

'Mech Bay

This huge building has six 'Mech bays and a repair platform, as well as a heavy-duty lift to the underground ammo storage and parts bays. The Pit is equipped to reload, retrofit, and repair, all at reasonable rates.

Observation Towers

These massive pillars rise far above the arena, providing a bird's-eye view of the action. Each of the four towers has an elevator that carries spectators to the shielded viewing platforms and is equipped with trivid cameras. Each platform can hold four viewers comfortably. The arena is used mainly for practice and other non-spectator matches.

Office

This small building contains the arena office complex and a viewing room where tapes of the matches can be reviewed and the participants debriefed. Anton lives on-site in the upstairs apartment. His quarters are secure and very comfortable.

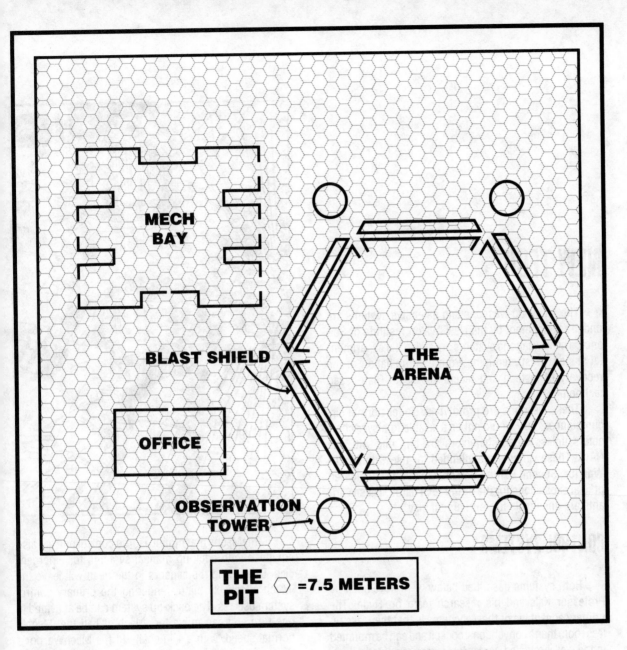

MECH BAY

BLAST SHIELD

THE ARENA

OFFICE

OBSERVATION TOWER

THE PIT ⬡ **=7.5 METERS**

CHARACTERS

Anton Hughes (Operator)

A meticulously efficient manager, Mr. Hughes is a consummate professional. His white suit and tie are always immaculate, and though he is not a vain man, he never has a hair out of place. Precision guides every facet of his life, making even his speech patterns slow and deliberate.

Anton is a hard man to get to know, but an easy man to work with. He maintains an emotional detachment from his work which can make him seem quite cold at times.

Vincent Amadore (Chief Tech)

The "Vin Man" is a cliche, and he knows it and enjoys it. Centuries ago, he would have been into cars instead of 'Mechs. His sleeveless black shirts, gold chains, and greased-back hair all attest to his wholehearted acceptance of an obsolete cultural archetype.

Vince is an expert tech, with years of experience to his credit, though he tends to add unapproved options to 'Mechs in his care, such as sound systems, excessive exterior lights, and tinted viewports. His own 'Mech, a customized *Hunchback*, has chromed armor and fuzzy dice in the cockpit.

NEW TECH

The following weapons and defensive systems are under development by the New Avalon Institute of Science. These weapons systems are still in the experimental stages, most stemming from a combination of the recovery of lostech and recent access to Clan-based technology.

These weapons are prototypes. Under normal circumstances, they would not be available to player characters unless those characters are affiliated with the NAIS. These variants are intended for use with **MechWarrior, Second Edition,** and should not be considered official expansions for the **BattleTech** game. These variants are unsuitable for tournament play.

CONTROL SYSTEMS

Both systems described below were developed by Professor Kale and his research team on Hyde. The primary advantage of these systems is that they take up less room than a conventional cockpit and can be mounted in the well-protected center torso area of a 'Mech.

General Game Notes

When either of these cockpit pods is mounted in the torso, the cockpit itself takes up one location, and a special life-support module takes up another. The two life-support locations normally positioned in the head must be split between the left and right torso. The three slots freed up in the head may mount anything the engineer desires. All weight considerations are the same as in a conventional cockpit. The eject system must be adapted to the new location, but functions identically to those in conventional cockpits.

BattleMechs that mount a torso control pod are also equipped with back-up manual systems for emergencies. Destroying the sensors in the head will leave the 'Mech effectively blind, rendering the primary control system useless. The back-up system can be activated in one turn and can move the 'Mech at half the 'Mech's normal speed, with a +3 penalty to the MechWarrior's Gunnery and Piloting skills.

General Glitch

A hit to any of the three life-support locations knocks out the entire life-support system permanently, and the MechWarrior takes one point of damage every turn for every five points of heat the BattleMech has built up at the end of the heat phase. (Or 1 point for every 20 points of heat in the Dueling system.) For example, a 'Mech that builds up 12 points of heat during the heat phase would inflict 2 points of damage on its hapless pilot that turn, a result of the proximity of the cockpit to the 'Mech's fusion reactors.

TORSO COCKPIT (EXTERNAL)

MODIFIED EJECT SYSTEM

TORSO COCKPIT (INTERNAL)

NEW TECH

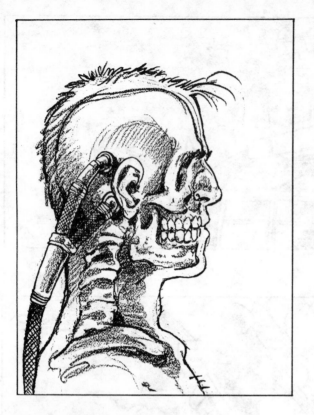

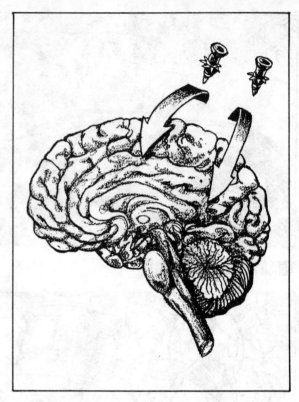

DIRECT NEURAL INTERFACE (DNI)

The concept behind DNI is simply to create a link between man and machine. Normally, the neurohelmet "reads" the neurological impulses of the region of the MechWarrior's brain that controls motor skills and balance. This constantly resets the 'Mech's gyro, effectively making the MechWarrior the 'Mech's inner ear.

This variant control system establishes a direct link between the pilot's nervous system and the BattleMech's control systems, allowing the MechWarrior to control the 'Mech as if it were his own body. This provides greater speed, agility, and accuracy than a standard interface.

As of 3053, however, biotechnology has yet to catch up even to the Star League-era level, which was itself not advanced enough to support an interface of this kind. Professor Kale has made some significant breakthroughs, but his system is inherently flawed.

Game Notes

A MechWarrior using a DNI system receives a –2 to his Gunnery Skill and a –3 to his Piloting Skill. If the Initiative rules from **Solaris VII** are used, the DNI also confers a +4 Initiative bonus.

Glitch

Kale's DNI system requires a surgically implanted interface connection. This factor alone makes the new system impractical for widespread application, as the surgery itself is experimental and somewhat dangerous. Once the connection is in place, however, it is easier to use than a bulky neurohelmet.

A second problem with the professor's interface is that he has been unable to develop effective buffers to damper the signal flowing from the 'Mech to the warrior. This creates a sensory overload that so far can only be countered by a drug called XA-3, created by Dr. Hunsaker. Even with the drug, prolonged exposure to the unfiltered signal can cause permanent nerve damage, insanity, and eventually death.

Without XA-3, feedback caused by damage to the BattleMech is dangerous and potentially lethal. A normal neurohelmet causes 1 point of damage to the warrior when the 'Mech's head is hit. A MechWarrior using DNI takes 1 point of damage *every time* the 'Mech is hit, even if the hit does not penetrate the armor.

The most insidious danger to the MechWarrior is that both DNI and XA-3 have proven addictive and can lead to obsessive and dangerous behavior on the part of the afflicted individual. It is possible to overcome the addictive side effects, but only by discontinuing use and enduring an extensive, painful withdrawal.

VIRTUAL REALITY PILOTING POD (VRPP)

In many ways, the VRPP is a scaled-down version of the more ambitious DNI system. Instead of a direct link to the pilot's nervous system, the VRPP uses an advanced version of the sensors in standard neurohelmets to feed control data to the BattleMech's navigation computers.

VRPP uses a modified neurohelmet in place of the surgical implant required for DNI. Unlike standard neurohelmets, the virtual-reality helmet is integral to the cockpit pod, and is lowered into position with the MechWarrior in the pod.

Instead of the standard direct-view and head-up displays, the virtual-reality interface displays piloting data in a wraparound display in the helmet's visor.

A virtual reality is a synthetic, computer-generated simulation of the BattleMech's exterior environment composed from sensor data. As a torso-mounted cockpit has no windows, this view is the only way for the MechWarrior to perceive the world around him.

Game Notes

A MechWarrior using a VRPP system receives a –1 to his Gunnery Skill and a –2 to his Piloting Skill. If the Initiative rules from **Solaris VII** are used, the VRPP also confers a +3 Initiative bonus.

Glitch

The virtual-reality control system is very different from conventional cockpit controls and takes some getting used to. Player characters will be unfamiliar with the VRPP controls, and so receive a +2 penalty to their Gunnery and Piloting skills. However, the player characters will still receive the benefits of the system, for a net modifier of +1 Gunnery and +0 to Piloting. At least one full day of intense training is required for characters to familiarize themselves with the system.

ALTERNATIVE ORDNANCE

The Tommyknockers Project is coordinated by Dr. James Long and is dedicated to developing a wide range of missile variants. While Dr. Long is in charge of several projects personally, he also has overall control of NAIS offensive ordnance research. In the game, treat these variants as standard missiles for purposes of tonnage and critical-hit locations, except that half as many missiles are available per ton of ammo (round down).

AX (ACID) WARHEAD

This variant warhead for short-range missiles is fitted with a chemical that becomes a highly corrosive acid when exposed to ferro-fibrous armor.

Game Notes

AX-equipped missiles do three points of damage against BattleMechs equipped with ferro-fibrous armor, but only one point against conventional armor and internal structures. Damage caused by an AX missile against ferro-fibrous armor may not be transferred to internal structures.

If the AX missiles are detonated in an ammo explosion each missile does one point of damage.

Glitch

The liquid contents of the AX warhead cause serious stabilization problems the NAIS has yet to overcome. Short-range missiles fitted with this variant are unbalanced and add a –2 penalty to the roll to determine how many missiles hit. Any roll less than 2 means that all the missiles missed their target.

RS (RETRO-STREAK) WARHEAD

The initial prototype of this missile warhead was originally designed by House Kurita forces, but variants can be found in the Federated Commonwealth and the Free Worlds League, usually in testing or as prototypes. NAIS began work two years ago on their own variant of this warhead.

Game Notes

This variant warhead for the Streak Missile Launcher feeds back the Streak Targeting Signal and redirects incoming Streak warheads. Any BattleMech equipped with the Retro-Streak system that is targeted and locked onto by Streak SRMs automatically fires one of these missiles.

The Streak's lock signal will lock onto and follow the Retro-Streak warhead.

Streak SRMs countered by a Retro-Streak warhead must roll for the number of missiles that hit, as with normal SRMs. Add a –2 modifier to all rolls when determining the number of missiles that hit a target. Any roll less than 2 indicates that all the missiles missed their target. (This bonus accounts for the fact that some of the missiles, confused by the bouncing signals, will simply never reach their targets.)

TC (TANDEM-CHARGE) WARHEAD

The SLDF originally began experimenting with the tandem-charge warhead system several years prior to Kerensky's Exodus. Some of these prototypes have been uncovered in caches discovered by units such as the Gray Death Legion and Snord's Irregulars.

Game Notes

These short-range missile warheads contain two charges that punch a controlled hole in armor to damage internal components. Damage done by this missile is allocated as one point of damage to armor, and one point to the internal structure of the target area. If the targeted area has no armor, the missile still does only one point of damage to the internal structure because of the narrow impact area of the shaped charge.

For ammunition explosions, treat each TC-equipped missile in a rack as a potential three points of damage.

LI (LASER INHIBITING) WARHEAD

This weapon is a by-product of experiments at the New Avalon Institute of Science, and is being fieldtested with a number of front-line units along the Periphery. The laser-inhibiting warhead is considered one of the best defensive missile delivery systems designed to date.

Game Notes

The LI warhead for the Arrow IV system is fired like a conventional missile, releasing a laser-inhibiting cloud of gas with intense prismatic qualities that diffuses laser attacks. The cloud affects the target hex and all surrounding hexes, has Level 2 elevation, and impairs visibility in the same manner as smoke.

MechWarriors firing any laser-based weapon through the cloud must apply a −2 penalty to damage for each hex of laser-inhibiting cloud through which the weapon is fired. While the laser-inhibiting gas limits damage on both sides of the battle, the advantage is to the 'Mech that fired the LI warhead, because that pilot will immediately switch to another form of attack.

Glitch

The laser-inhibiting gas cloud rises quickly, giving it a higher elevation than smoke, but the cloud dissipates in two rounds.

FTL (FOLLOW THE LEADER) WARHEAD

The Follow-the-Leader missile warhead is derived from lostech dating back to the Star League era. Recent recoveries of the lost technology have allowed almost all Inner Sphere Houses to begin experimenting with variant models of this missile class. Thus far, only the NAIS Tommyknockers Project has achieved any long-standing success in testing the system.

Game Notes

When using the FTL warhead variant for LRMs, the player rolls to hit as if firing a normal missile barrage. Each missile in this system will impact on the same location. For example, if an LRM-20 missile rack fires and twelve missiles hit, if the first missile hits the targeted 'Mech's right leg, all twelve missiles hit in the right leg, doing twelve points of damage.

Glitch

The target acquisition system of FTL warheads must lock on to the first missile in the barrage that hits the designated target. Sometimes the system will choose a missile which has missed as the lead missile, causing the entire flight to miss. This translates into a net +2 Fire Modifier.

HS (HEAT SEEKING) WARHEAD

The HS targeting warheads were originally created by the Federated Commonwealth for testing in the War of 3039, and subsequently were found in the hands of the Draconis Combine, as well. The Clans have not used this system, and Clan warriors who have fought against MechWarriors using the HS warheads consider these weapons dishonorable.

Game Notes

HS warheads are fitted on standard short-range missiles, but because of the elaborate targeting mechanism, carry less explosive, doing only one point of damage instead of the normal two. HS missiles receive a bonus equal to the target 'Mech's Fire Modifier from heat build-up (if any). If the missiles hit a location containing a heat sink, any critical hits automatically destroy heat sinks before any other critical location.

Glitch

HS warheads use hot points such as heat sinks for target acquisition. If the targeted 'Mech has no heat build-up, it is very difficult for the warhead to achieve a lock-on, resulting in a +2 Fire Modifier.

SS (SHOOT AND SIT) WARHEAD

The Shoot and Sit warheads for the Narc missile-launcher do not explode on impact, but attach themselves to the exterior of the targeted BattleMech. The MechWarrior who fired the missiles may then detonate them at any time. Dr. Long feels that the warheads, in the hands of the right MechWarrior, can be an effective weapon.

One possible tactic for using this missile is to hit a targeted BattleMech with several volleys of missiles, then detonate all the missiles at once. In theory, the amount of damage done in a single turn by simultaneously exploding all the warheads should be enough to knock down the targeted BattleMech.

Game Notes

The player character firing the SS warheads should make his normal To Hit and Damage Location rolls, keeping track of the number of missiles attached to the BattleMech and where each missile is located. The firing player may detonate all of the missiles on a single enemy 'Mech at any time during any subsequent Combat Phase. The missiles may not be detonated separately; the detonation signal will automatically explode all attached missiles.

SS warheads do 3 points of damage each when they are detonated, and inflict 3 points of damage each in an ammo explosion. Note that if the missiles attach to a limb, and the limb is blown off later in combat, any unexploded missiles on that limb are lost and cannot inflict further damage to the targeted BattleMech.

Glitch

Any time a location with active SS warheads is hit, roll one die for each warhead. On a roll of 1 or 2, the warhead falls off or is destroyed. On a result of 6, the warhead is prematurely detonated, adding its 3 points of damage to the attack.

NEW WEAPONS SYSTEMS

BUZZSAW

This weapon is a circular saw-blade mounted in place of a hand on a BattleMech. This weapons system was built for close combat, allowing the attacker to maim the opposing BattleMech using the specially hardened and sharpened saw blades to cut through armor.

Game Notes

This device weighs four tons and takes up two critical-hit locations. Using the buzzsaw generates 3 points of heat. This weapon is used in physical combat to inflict 2D6 points of damage. The nature of the weapon prevents a BattleMech outfitted with the buzzsaw from having a hand or hand actuator on the arm where the buzzsaw is mounted.

Glitch

The buzzsaw blade is relatively fragile. An attack roll of 2 for the buzzsaw shatters the weapon and renders it useless until the blade can be replaced.

THUNDERBOLT

This weapon is a one-shot ground-to-ground missile. This weapon delivers a chemical blast, generating a lot of heat when fired, and an even greater amount of heat and explosive damage to its target.

Game Notes

The Thunderbolt missile can be mounted on the right or left torso of a BattleMech, weighs 1 ton, and occupies one critical-hit location. The Thunderbolt does the same damage and has the same range modifiers as an AC10, and generates 6 points of heat when launched.

Glitch

Thunderbolt missiles are very dangerous in an ammo explosion, doing 10 points of damage and generating 15 points of additional heat.

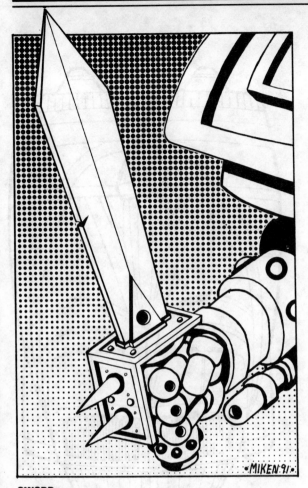

Game Notes

The self-destruct device weighs one ton, takes up one critical-hit location, and must be located in either the left or right torso. When activated, anything in the BattleMech's hex is destroyed and anything in the surrounding hexes sustains damage equal to the BattleMech's Engine Rating divided by 15.

Glitch

When the device is used, the BattleMech is destroyed. If the MechWarrior attempts to eject when the device is used, the player must roll two dice with a –1 modifier for each point of damage the MechWarrior has sustained. If the total is 3 or more, the MechWarrior escapes the cockpit of the BattleMech alive. Any other result means the MechWarrior dies in the explosion.

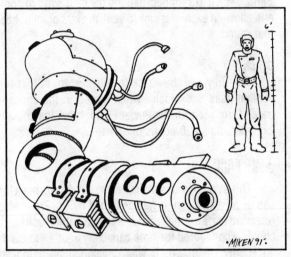

SB (SILVER BULLET) GAUSS

This project is a variant on the Gauss rifle that projects a burst of shrapnel, rather than a massive slug of nickel ferrous metal. This explosive is primarily geared toward anti-Elemental attacks, but is also effective against BattleMechs and other vehicles, distributing the damage done by a normal Gauss rifle attack to multiple target areas.

Game Notes

Silver Bullet refers to the Gauss rifle ammunition. While it has the same weight restrictions as normal ammunition, it delivers damage differently. A Silver Bullet round inflicts damage in the same manner as an LRM-15. The damage roll is is broken up into 5-point increments when determining location.

Glitch

Like normal Gauss rifles, the SB Gauss will explode if hit, but the SB ammo will also explode if hit, doing 15 points of damage per round still unfired.

SWORD

In recent years, NAIS has shown a strong interest in 'Mech-held weaponry. The Excalibur Project is further proof of that interest, developed by the team that designed the *Hatchetman* and the *Axeman*. This weapon system provides a sword designed specifically for BattleMechs.

Game Notes

The weapon is used in physical combat in the same manner as the axe and hatchet mechanisms. The sword does only punch damage, but confers a –2 bonus to the attack roll because of the added reach. The Excalibur system weighs 1 ton for every 20 tons that the Battle-Mech weighs.

SELF DESTRUCT

This device is a one-shot, desperation, last-ditch device a BattleMech pilot can use to create wide-spread destruction. When activated, the device cuts all fuel controls, dumping all remaining fuel into the power plant, and breaks open the magnetic containment of the power plant. The resulting engine flare creates a fireball that consumes the 'Mech and anything nearby.

NEW DEFENSIVE SYSTEMS

This staff is jointly managed by Dr. Antonio Priar and Dr. Boyd Petersen. The goal of this research staff is to investigate defensive systems to counter the advances in offensive BattleTechnology.

COOLANT SYSTEM

Project Power Flush is a one-shot emergency cooling system. The coolant system takes up 1 critical-hit location and weighs 1 ton.

Game Notes

When activated, an ultracool gas is forced into the BattleMech's extremities, bathing the heat sinks in coolant, allowing each heat sink to vent an extra point of heat that round.

Glitch

The only real drawback to this system is that the coolant itself is explosive when stored in the concentrated form used for the Power Flush. If hit, the coolant explodes, doing 20 points of damage.

JUMP PACK

This system is an attachable one-shot jump pack for use by a BattleMech. It was designed by Dr. Priar, who reasoned that a normally ground-bound BattleMech force could be configured for jump capability in order to catch an enemy off guard. It was developed as a logical extension of the modular BattleTechnology used by the Clans.

Game Notes

When activated, this system gives the BattleMech a single jump. The jump range is determined by subtracting 1 from a base of 9 for each 10 tons of BattleMech weight over 40 tons (rounded down). For example, a 50-ton *Hunchback* would have a jump movement of 8. Heat is generated as normal for a jump.

When the device has been used, it is automatically ejected to allow normal movement.

Glitch

The bulk of the system, mounted on the back and legs of the 'Mech, reduces the base ground movement of the 'Mech to half normal.

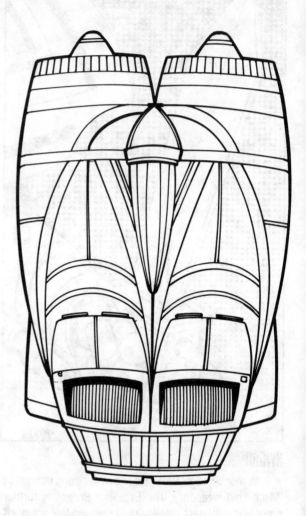

BLUE SHIELD PROJECT

This system is a concentrated particle-field damper, which absorbs and disperses the energy of incoming PPC fire.

Game Notes

The Blue Shield project requires 3 tons of space and occupies one critical-hit space in each of the 'Mech's locations. The system halves all damage by PPCs against the BattleMech equipped with the device. Destroying any of the shield's critical locations destroys the entire shield.

Glitch

Every time the Blue Shield is activated, roll two die. On a result of 2, the system overloads, destroying all the shield critical locations and inflicting 5 points of internal damage on each of the BattleMech's locations.

NEW BATTLEMECHS

P1-WF WILDFIRE

Overview

As the VRPP project neared completion, a Battle-Mech was designed to incorporate the new technology. Based on the 3050 *Crusader*, the new *Wildfire* would be the first completely headless BattleMech. Two proto-types were custom-built in a special factory in the NAIS facility on Hyde.

Early testing has shown the prototype BattleMech to be everything its designers hoped. The VRPP control system has been successfully integrated, giving the *Wildfire* unparalleled agility, and prospects for success-ful mass production of this design are excellent.

Capabilities

In addition to the prototype control system, this BattleMech takes full advantage of other recent techno-logical developments, including Endo Steel internal struc-ture, an XL engine, ferro-fibrous armor, and weapons systems such as Streak SRMs and large pulse lasers.

This well-armored 'Mech is designed to offer a lot of firepower at short range, and provides the speed and maneuverability to close quickly. The *Wildfire* is intended for use as a pursuit 'Mech, and so its effectiveness drops off at long range. This is an advantage in the arenas.

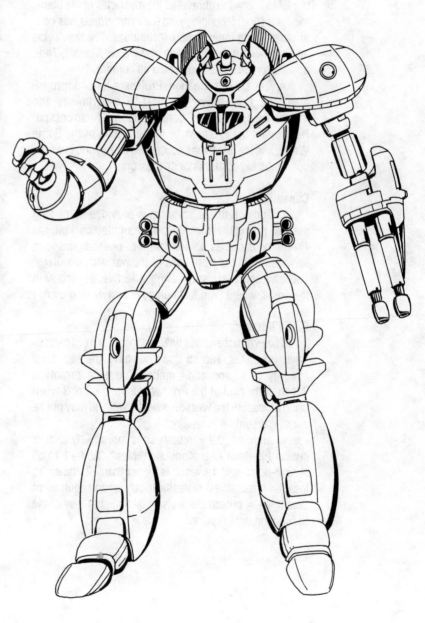

Type: **P1-Wildfire**			*Tons*
Tonnage:	65		
Internal Structure			3.25
Engine:	Magna	23	
Walking MP:	6		
Running MP:	9		
Heat Sinks:	13		3
Gyro:			4
Cockpit:			3
Armor Factor:	197		11

	Internal Structure	Armor Value
Head:	3	9
Center Torso:	21	33/9
R/L Torso:	15	24/6
R/L Arm:	10	20
R/L Leg:	15	23

Weapons and Ammo:

Type	Location	Critical	Tons
SRM 2 Streak	RL	1	1.5
SRM 2 Streak	LL	1	1.5
Ammo Streak (50)	RT	1	1
Large Pulse Laser	RA	2	7
Medium Pulse Laser	LA	1	2
CASE	RT	1	1
Ammo MG (200)	RT	1	1
Machine Gun	RA	1	0.5
Small Pulse Laser	RA	1	1

PROMETHEUS

Overview

This one-of-a-kind 'Mech was created by one of the NAIS research teams assigned to study Clan technology. It will never see mass production or even duplication.

The *Prometheus* was an attempt to construct a new BattleMech from salvaged Clan materiel. Unfortunately, the NAIS has yet to unravel all the mysteries of the Clans' modular (pod) technology, so the *Prometheus* was constructed using Inner Sphere techniques. The result was an ungainly but deadly fusion of the *Loki*, *Madcat*, *Thor*, and *Vulture* that easily defeated all comers.

A year after its creation, Professor Kale "appropriated" the *Prometheus* for his DNI experiments and installed one of the VRPP control pods in a torso cockpit. He brought the *Prometheus* to the arenas of the Game World, and the 'Mech has succeeded far beyond even the optimistic expectations of its creators.

Capabilities

In addition to the advantages provided by placing the DNI pod in the 'Mech's torso-mounted cockpit, the *Prometheus* carries a wide range of unusual weapons salvaged from the front lines of the war with the Clans. These weapons are surprisingly effective, especially in the arena, where Clan technology is largely unknown.

Game Notes

The *Prometheus* was tinkered together from parts of other machines, and so does not have the structural integrity of a production model or even a prototype 'Mech. If the pilot of the *Prometheus* rolls a 2 or 3 when firing a weapon, the weapon is destroyed and may not be used again until it is repaired.

In addition, the *Prometheus* is more likely to take critical hits than is a production 'Mech. Add +1 to all critical-hit rolls. If the result is higher than 12, the entire location is destroyed. Note that locations and equipment destroyed by critical hits are salvageable, but they cease to function until repaired.

Type: **Prometheus**			Tons
Tonnage:		75	75
Internal Structure			3.75
Engine:		375 GM	19.25
Walking MP:		5	
Running MP:		8	
Heat Sinks:		13	3
Gyro:			4
Cockpit:			3
Armor Factor:		206	11.5

	Internal Structure	Armor Value
Head:	3	8
Center Torso:	23	35/9
R/L Torso:	16	25/7
R/L Arm:	12	17
R/L Leg:	16	28

Weapons and Ammo:

Type	Location	Critical	Tons
LRM 15	LT	1	3.5
Ammo LRM 15 (8)	LT	1	1
LRM 15	RT	1	3.5
Ammo LRM 15 (8)	RT	1	1
SRM 6	LT	1	1.5
Ammo SRM 6 (15)	LT	1	1
SRM 6	RT	1	1.5
Ammo SRM 6 (15)	RT	1	1
Machine Gun	LT	1	0.25
Machine Gun	LT	1	0.25
Machine Gun	LT	1	0.25
Machine Gun	RT	1	0.25
Machine Gun	RT	1	0.25
Machine Gun	RT	1	0.25
Ammo MG (200)	H	1	1
ER PPC	RA	2	6
Large Pulse Laser	LA	2	6
Medium Pulse Laser	LA	1	2

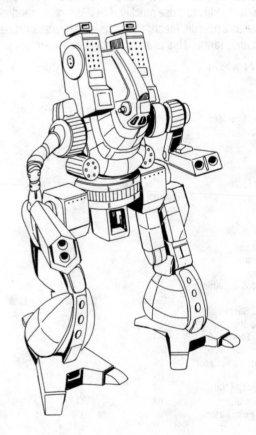

EPIMETHEUS

Overview

Professor Kale began working on the *Epimetheus* shortly after the retrofit of the *Prometheus* was finished. Dissatisfied with the performance of his patchwork 'Mech, the brilliant scientist and his hand-picked research team began designing a new 'Mech, incorporating the modular Clan systems into a basic Inner Sphere design.

When Kale fled the Dark Mirage facility on Hyde, he took the half-finished *Epimetheus* prototype and sufficient materiel to complete the BattleMech at his new base on Solaris VII. Final assembly took several months in the converted pumping station that served as his stable.

Because of the materiel and expertise required to build this 'Mech, the *Epimetheus* will probably never see production, despite the fact that all the design work and testing has been done. The only logical site for such an effort would be an Inner Sphere factory that has been converted by the Clans for their own use, and they are unlikely to surrender one for a joint manufacturing effort.

Capabilities

The *Epimetheus* is a sound but untested design incorporating the best of Inner Sphere and Clan technology and the DNI control system, creating a machine that is faster, more powerful, and easier to pilot and control than any known 'Mech.

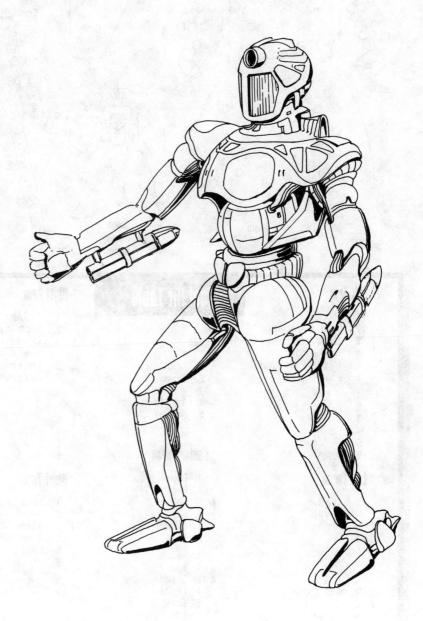

Type: **Epimetheus**			*Tons*
Tonnage:			80
Internal Structure			4.5
Engine:		400XL	26.25
Walking MP:		5	
Running MP:		8	
Heat Sinks:		10	0
Gyro:			4
Cockpit:			3
Armor Factor:		221	11.5

	Internal Structure	Armor Value
Head:	3	7
Center Torso:	25	35/15
R/L Torso:	17	21/13
R/L Arm:	13	21
R/L Leg:	17	27

Weapons and Ammo:

Type	Location	Critical	Tons
Heat Sinks	RT	6	3
Ultra AC/10	H	4	10
Targeting Computer	LT	5	5
ER Large Laser	LA	2	4
ER Large Laser	RA	2	4
Medium Pulse Laser	LA	1	2
Medium Pulse Laser	RA	1	2

BATTLETECH®

Armor Diagram

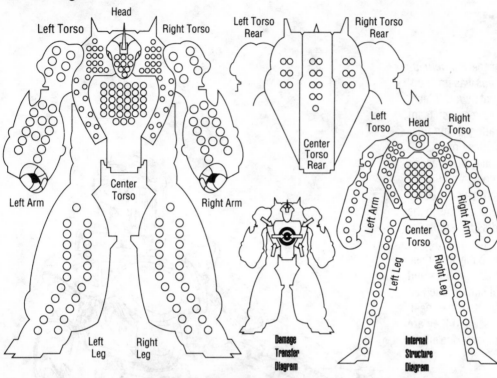

Head

Left Torso • Right Torso

Left Arm • Center Torso • Right Arm

Left Leg • Right Leg

Left Torso Rear • Right Torso Rear

Center Torso Rear

Left Torso • Head • Right Torso

Left Arm • Center Torso • Right Arm

Left Leg • Right Leg

Damage Transfer Diagram

Internal Structure Diagram

Mech Data

Type: WILDFIRE
Tonnage: **65**
Movement Points:
  Walking: **6**
  Running: **9**
  Jumping: **0**

Weapons Inventory

#	Type	Location
1	SRM 2 Streak	RL
1	SRM 2 Streak	LL
1	Large Pulse Laser	RA
1	Medium Pulse Laser	LA
1	CASE	RT
1	Machine Gun	RA
1	Small Pulse Laser	RA

AMMO:
  Streak (50)
  MG (200)

Total Heat Sinks

◯◯◯◯◯◯◯◯◯◯   Double
◯◯◯

Warrior Data

Name: _____
Gunnery Skill: _____
Piloting Skill: _____
Hits Taken: (Consciousness Number)

1st	2nd	3rd	4th	5th	6th
(3)	(5)	(7)	(10)	(11)	(Dead)

Critical Hit Table

Left Arm

1
1. Shoulder
2. Upper Arm Actuator
3. Lower Arm Actuator
4. Hand Actuator
5. Medium Pulse Laser
6. Roll Again

2
1. Roll Again
2. Roll Again
3. Roll Again
4. Roll Again
5. Roll Again
6. Roll Again

Left Torso

1
1. Life Support
2. Roll Again
3. Roll Again
4. Roll Again
5. Roll Again
6. Roll Again

2
1. Roll Again
2. Roll Again
3. Roll Again
4. Roll Again
5. Roll Again
6. Roll Again

Left Leg

1. Hip
2. Upper Leg Actuator
3. Lower Leg Actuator
4. Foot Actuator
5. SRM 2 (Streak)
6. Roll Again

Head

1. Roll Again
2. Sensors
3. Roll Again
4. Anti-Missile System
5. Sensors
6. Roll Again

Center Torso

1
1. Engine
2. Engine
3. Engine
4. Gyro
5. Gyro
6. Gyro

2
1. Gyro
2. Engine
3. Engine
4. Engine
5. Cockpit
6. Life Support

Engine Hits	◯◯◯
Gyro Hits	◯◯
Sensor Hits	◯◯

Right Arm

1
1. Shoulder
2. Upper Arm Actuator
3. Lower Arm Actuator
4. Small Pulse Laser
5. Large Pulse Laser
6. Large Pulse Laser

2
1. MG
2. Roll Again
3. Roll Again
4. Roll Again
5. Roll Again
6. Roll Again

Right Torso

1
1. Life Support
2. Ammo (SRM2) 50
3. Ammo (MG) 200
4. Ammo (AMS) 12
5. CASE
6. Roll Again

2
1. Roll Again
2. Roll Again
3. Roll Again
4. Roll Again
5. Roll Again
6. Roll Again

Right Leg

1. Hip
2. Upper Leg Actuator
3. Lower Leg Actuator
4. Foot Actuator
5. SRM 2 (Streak)
6. Roll Again

Heat Scale

30	Shutdown
29	
28	Ammo Explosion, avoid on 8+
27	
26	Shutdown, avoid on 10+
25	-5 Movement Points
24	+4 Modifier to Fire
23	Ammo Explosion, avoid on 6+
22	Shutdown, avoid on 8+
21	
20	-4 Movement Points
19	Ammo Explosion, avoid on 4+
18	Shutdown, avoid on 6+
17	+3 Modifier to Fire
16	
15	-3 Movement Points
14	Shutdown, avoid on 4+
13	+2 Modifier to fire
12	
11	
10	-2 Movement Points
09	
08	+1 Modifier to Fire
07	
06	
05	-1 Movement Points
04	
03	
02	
01	
00	

FASA CORPORATION

BATTLETECH is a Registered Trademark of FASA Corporation. Copyright 1991. Permission to photocopy for personal use.

BATTLETECH®

Armor Diagram

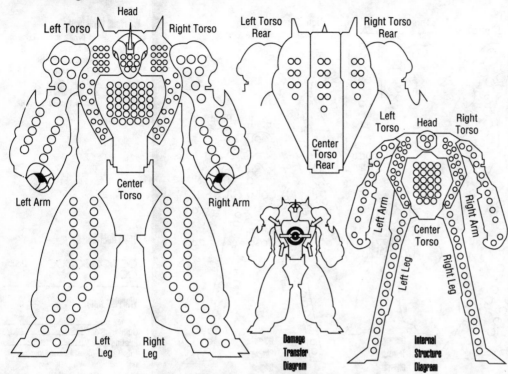

Left Torso — Head — Right Torso
Left Arm — Center Torso — Right Arm
Left Leg — Right Leg

Left Torso Rear — Right Torso Rear — Center Torso Rear

Left Torso — Head — Right Torso
Left Arm — Center Torso — Right Arm
Left Leg — Right Leg

Damage Transfer Diagram

Internal Structure Diagram

Mech Data

Type: **PROMETHEUS**
Tonnage: **75**
Movement Points:
 Walking: **5**
 Running: **8**
 Jumping: **0**

Weapons Inventory

#	Type	Location
1	LRM 15	LT
1	LRM 15	RT
1	SRM 6	LT
1	SRM 6	RT
3	Machine Gun	LT
3	Machine Gun	RT
1	ER PPC	RA
1	Large Pulse Laser	LA
1	Medium Pulse Laser	LA

AMMO:
 LRM 15 (8)
 LRM 15 (8)
 SRM 6 (15)
 SRM 6 (15)
 MG (200)

Total Heat Sinks

 Double

Warrior Data

Name: _____
Gunnery Skill: _____
Piloting Skill: _____
Hits Taken: (Consciousness Number)

1st	2nd	3rd	4th	5th	6th
(3)	(5)	(7)	(10)	(11)	(Dead)

Critical Hit Table

Left Arm

1
1. Shoulder
2. Upper Arm Actuator
3. Lower Arm Actuator
4. Roll Again
5. Large Pulse Laser
6. Large Pulse Laser

2
1. Medium Pulse Laser
2. Roll Again
3. Ferro-Fibrous
4. Endo-Steel
5. Roll Again
6. Roll Again

Left Torso

1
1. Life Suppoer
2. XL Engine
3. XL Engine
4. Ferro-Fibrous
5. LRM 15
6. Ammo (LRM 15) 8

2
1. SRM 6
2. Ammo (SRM 6) 15
3. Machine Gun
4. Machine Gun
5. Machine Gun
6. Endo-Steel

Left Leg
1. Hip
2. Upper Leg Actuator
3. Lower Leg Actuator
4. Foot Actuator
5. Ferro-Fibrous
6. Endo-Steel

Head
1. Ferro-Fibrous
2. Sensors
3. Endo-Steel
4. Ammo (MG) 200
5. Sensors
6. Roll Again

Center Torso

1
1. Engine
2. Engine
3. Engine
4. Gyro
5. Gyro
6. Gyro

2
1. Gyro
2. Engine
3. Engine
4. Engine
5. Cockpit
6. Life Support

Engine Hits ○○○
Gyro Hits ○○○
Sensor Hits ○○

Right Arm

1
1. Shoulder
2. Upper Arm Actuator
3. Lower Arm Actuator
4. Roll Again
5. ER PPC
6. ER PPC

2
1. Roll Again
2. Ferro-Fibrous
3. Endo-Steel
4. Roll Again
5. Roll Again
6. Roll Again

Right Torso

1
1. Life Support
2. XL Engine
3. XL Engine
4. Ferro-Fibrous
5. LRM 15
6. Ammo (LRM 15) 8

2
1. SRM 6
2. Ammo (SRM 6) 15
3. Machine Gun
4. Machine Gun
5. Machine Gun
6. Endo-Steel

Right Leg
1. Hip
2. Upper Leg Actuator
3. Lower Leg Actuator
4. Foot Actuator
5. Ferro-Fibrous
6. Endo-Steel

Heat Scale

30	Shutdown
29	
28	Ammo Explosion, avoid on 8+
27	
26	Shutdown, avoid on 10+
25	-5 Movement Points
24	+4 Modifier to Fire
23	Ammo Explosion, avoid on 6+
22	Shutdown, avoid on 8+
21	
20	-4 Movement Points
19	Ammo Explosion, avoid on 4+
18	Shutdown, avoid on 6+
17	+3 Modifier to Fire
16	
15	-3 Movement Points
14	Shutdown, avoid on 4+
13	+2 Modifier to fire
12	
11	
10	-2 Movement Points
09	
08	+1 Modifier to Fire
07	
06	
05	-1 Movement Points
04	
03	
02	
01	
00	

BATTLETECH is a Registered Trademark of FASA Corporation. Copyright 1991. Permission to photocopy for personal use.

BATTLETECH®

Armor Diagram

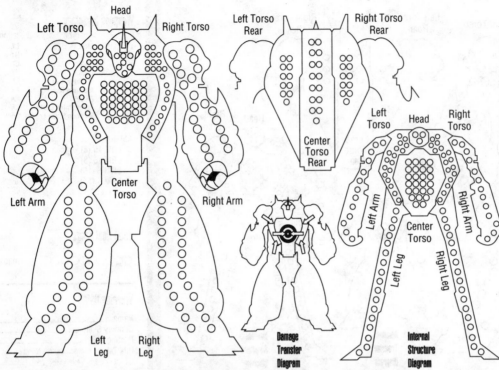

Head

Left Torso · Right Torso

Left Torso Rear · Right Torso Rear

Center Torso Rear

Left Arm · Center Torso · Right Arm

Left Leg · Right Leg

Left Torso · Head · Right Torso

Left Arm · Center Torso · Right Arm

Left Leg · Right Leg

Damage Transfer Diagram

Internal Structure Diagram

Mech Data

Type: **EPIMETHEUS**
Tonnage: **80**
Movement Points:
Walking: **5**
Running: **8**
Jumping: **4**

Weapons Inventory

#	Type	Location
1	Ultra AC/10	H
1	Targeting Computer	LT
1	ER Large Laser	LA
1	ER Large Laser	RA
1	Medium Pulse Laser	L A
1	Medium Pulse Laser	RA

Total Heat Sinks

○○○○○○○○○○   Double
○○○

Warrior Data

Name: _____
Gunnery Skill: _____
Piloting Skill: _____
Hits Taken: (Consciousness Number)
1st 2nd 3rd 4th 5th 6th
(3) (5) (7) (10) (11) (Dead)

Critical Hit Table

Left Arm

1
1. Shoulder
2. Upper Arm Actuator
3. Lower Arm Actuator
4. Hand Actuator
5. Ferro-Fibrous
6. Ferro-Fibrous

2
1. ER Large Laser
2. ER Large Laser
3. Medium Pulse Laser
4. Roll Again
5. Roll Again
6. Roll Again

Left Torso

1
1. XL Engine
2. XL Engine
3. Life Support
4. Endo-Steel
5. Endo-Steel
6. Endo-Steel

2
1. Targeting Computer
2. Targeting Computer
3. Targeting Computer
4. Targeting Computer
5. Targeting Computer
6. Roll Again

Left Leg

1. Hip
2. Upper Leg Actuator
3. Lower Leg Actuator
4. Foot Actuator
5. Endo-Steel
6. Endo-Steel

Head

1. Sensors
2. Sensors
3. Ultra AC/10
4. Ultra AC/10
5. Ultra AC/10
6. Ultra AC/10

Center Torso

1
1. Engine
2. Engine
3. Engine
4. Gyro
5. Gyro
6. Gyro

2
1. Gyro
2. Engine
3. Engine
4. Engine
5. Life Support
6. Cockpit

Engine Hits ○○○
Gyro Hits ○○○
Sensor Hits ○○

Right Arm

1
1. Shoulder
2. Upper Arm Actuator
3. Lower Arm Actuator
4. Hand Actuator
5. Ferro-Fibrous
6. Ferro-Fibrous

2
1. ER Large Laser
2. ER Large Laser
3. Medium Pulse Laser
4. Roll Again
5. Roll Again
6. Roll Again

Right Torso

1
1. XL Engine
2. XL Engine
3. Life Support
4. Ferro-Fibrous
5. Ferro-Fibrous
6. Ferro-Fibrous

2
1. Heat Sink
2. Heat Sink
3. Heat Sink
4. Heat Sink
5. Heat Sink
6. Heat Sink

Right Leg

1. Hip
2. Upper Leg Actuator
3. Lower Leg Actuator
4. Foot Actuator
5. Endo-Steel
6. Endo-Steel

Heat Scale

30	Shutdown
29	
28	Ammo Explosion, avoid on 8+
27	
26	Shutdown, avoid on 10+
25	-5 Movement Points
24	+4 Modifier to Fire
23	Ammo Explosion, avoid on 6+
22	Shutdown, avoid on 8+
21	
20	-4 Movement Points
19	Ammo Explosion, avoid on 4+
18	Shutdown, avoid on 6+
17	+3 Modifier to Fire
16	
15	-3 Movement Points
14	Shutdown, avoid on 4+
13	+2 Modifier to fire
12	
11	
10	-2 Movement Points
09	
08	+1 Modifier to Fire
07	
06	
05	-1 Movement Points
04	
03	
02	
01	
00	

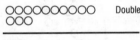

FASA CORPORATION

BATTLETECH is a Registered Trademark of FASA Corporation. Copyright 1991. Permission to photocopy for personal use

see the UNIVERSE
on 4/10ths of a cent a day!

COMMISSION ME AS A FULL MEMBER!

Now is your chance to get all of the latest information on the Inner Sphere, plus the latest news on FASA products and releases.

For only $16.00* a year you'll receive the following:
- the 24 page BATTLETECH MANUAL, packed with indispensible charts, forms and information on playing BattleTech:
  - Writer's Guidelines
  - Complete BattleTech Combat Values Listing featuring all available 'Mechs
  - Regional Map - to start your climb to the top of the Warrior ranking system.
  - Lance Control Mastersheet
  - Battle History Mastersheet
  - Engagement Mastersheet
  - Combat Loss Mastersheet
  - Battle Ranking Mastersheet
- Full Color BattleTech poster
- MECHFORCE NORTH AMERICA Identification Card
- MECHFORCE NORTH AMERICA Commission Certificate
- Four issues of MECH magazine - the hottest publication in the Inner Sphere.
  - Each quarter covers such topics as:
    - Major events in the Inner Sphere and beyond
    - New and Variant Mechs of the Clans and Houses
    - MechWarrior Fiction
    - BattleTech Scenarios
    - Battle Report - with the latest North American rankings for the best MechWarriors
    - Chapter Contacts - Find out who is playing near you
    - Reviews & Previews - read about FASA's hottest new projects - before they hit the stores
    - and much, much more...
- Ability to purchase from our exclusive "For Members Only" catalogue of MechForce Equipment:
  - Purchase back issues of MECH magazine
  - Special issues of MECH magazine
  - Laminated, multi-colored, double-sided Mastersheets
    - Aerotech Design Worksheet
    - Mech Design Worksheet
    - Vehicle Design Worksheet
    - Aerotech Clan Combat Control Sheet
    - Mech Clan Combat Control Sheet
    - Mech Inner Sphere Combat Control Sheet

BATTLETECH®, MECH®, BATTLEMECH®, MECHFORCE® AND MECHWARRIOR® ARE REGISTERED TRADEMARKS OF FASA CORPORATION. USED BY PERMISSION. ALL RIGHTS RESERVED. COPYRIGHT © 1991 FASA CORPORATION.

**THIS IS TOO GOOD TO BE TRUE! I ACCEPT YOUR CHALLENGE!
MAKE ME A FULL MEMBER OF MECHFORCE NORTH AMERICA!**

(RENEWALS, PLEASE INCLUDE OLD MEMBER/CHAPTER NUMBER)
_____

NAME: _____
ADDRESS (PLEASE PRINT)

HOUSE/CLAN AFFILIATION _____

STREET: _____
APT. OR ROUTE NUMBER _____

CITY: _____ STATE _____
ZIP CODE _____

PHONE NUMBER: _____

SEND CHECK OR MONEY ORDER ONLY TO:
MECHFORCE NORTH AMERICA
2101 WEST BROADWAY #305
PO BOX 6018
COLUMBIA, MO 65202-6018

CANADIAN, PUERTO RICAN, AND MEXICAN MEMBERS PLEASE ADD $4.00 SHIPPING & HANDLING. ALL OTHERS OUTSIDE THE UNITED STATES PLEASE ADD $6.00.

ON SALE NOW!

BATTLETECH®
SOLARIS VII
THE GAME WORLD

A CAMPAIGN SETTING FOR BATTLETECH AND MECHWARRIOR II

FASA CORPORATION

BATTLETECH® is a Registered Trademark of FASA Corporation. SOLARIS VII™ is a Trademark of FASA Corporation. Copyright © 1991 FASA Corporation. All Rights Reserved.